STILL
IN THE
STORM

FACING LIFE'S DISAPPOINTMENTS
WITH FRESH FAITH

JAMEY SANTO

FOREWORD BY DR. DAVE MARTIN

What Others Are Saying

Jamey Santo opens up the pages of his own life in this faith-building book *Still in the Storm*. Each page is packed with new covenant truth to stoke your faith as he shares the story of the sudden loss of his eight year old son Gavin and how his family clung to Christ as they faced the biggest storm of their lives. Your faith will be strengthened as you follow Jamey's journey, as he encourages you to take a look at your own life, and as you apply the principles found in each important chapter.

Ben Dailey | Lead Pastor/Author | Calvary Church | Irving-TX

In his incredible new book Jamey shows us critical keys to holding onto your faith in the toughest times. From his very own journey with his eight year old son who was diagnosed with brain cancer, we learn what it really means not just to lean on God, but to fully trust him.

Jim Raley | Lead Pastor/Author | Calvary Christian Center | Ormond Beach-FL

Still In The Storm is an incredibly timely and uplifting book full of insight and encouragement for your life. My friend, Jamey, walked through one of the most heart-breaking experiences with his family and has chosen to share the amazing revelations God strengthened him with through the journey. I promise this book will HELP you. Life can be overwhelming and fear-inducing, but Jamey's words bring amazing reminders that God is always with us, building our confidence in His faithfulness...even in the storm.

Daniel Eric Groves | Lead Pastor/Worship Artist | Anthem Of Hope Church | Columbus-OH

Still in the Storm reminds us that Jesus never leaves us or forsakes us, even when it seems like the waves of life are pounding us from every direction. There is no bigger storm that a father could possibly endure than the storm that unexpectedly hits his own child. Jamey Santo pours his heart onto the pages of this wonderful book, sharing the very personal story of his son's battle with brain cancer. Throughout this book you will discover important ways to build your faith even in the midst of life's greatest tragedy.

Bernie Moore | Evangelist | Bernie Moore Ministries | Frisco-TX

In life when something bad happens, it's not a time to blame God, it's a time to run to Him. I love *Still In The Storm* because it instils hope, renews your faith and gives you the steps you need to come out on top.

Anthony Shepherd | Worship Pastor | Church In The Son | Orlando-FL

This book will give you hope to trust God in the midst of any challenge. Jamey is a man of unswerving and uncompromising faith in God. He has turned that passion and life experience into the pages of this book to help us learn how to find faith and trust God in every season.

Caleb Wehrli | Lead Pastor | Victory Orlando | Orlando-FL

Have you ever felt like your life's storm was certainly going to be the end of you? Open your eyes to a perspective of faith! Jamey Santo shows us how to see and respond to all that is happening around us. This book is a roadmap to the inner calm necessary to endure any obstacle that impedes our victory. Turn the page and live!

Allen Griffin | Evangelist | Allen Griffin Ministries | Ormond Beach-FL

Scripture quotations marked (NIV) are taken from the Holy Bible, New International Version®, NIV®. Copyright © 1973, 1978, 1984, 2011 by Biblica, Inc.™ Used by permission of Zondervan. All rights reserved worldwide. www.zondervan.com. The "NIV" and "New International Version" are trademarks registered in the United States Patent and Trademark Office by Biblica, Inc.™

Scripture quotations marked NLT are taken from the Holy Bible, New Living Translation, copyright 1996, 2004, 2007 by Tyndale House Foundation. Used by permission of Tyndale House Publishers, Inc., Carol Stream, Illinois 60188. All rights reserved.

Scripture quotations marked (TLB) are taken from The Living Bible copyright © 1971. Used by permission of Tyndale House Publishers, Inc., Carol Stream, Illinois 60188. All rights reserved.

Scripture quotations from THE MESSAGE. Copyright © by Eugene H. Peterson 1993, 1994, 1995, 1996, 2000, 2001, 2002. Used by permission of Tyndale House Publishers, Inc.

Scripture taken from the New King James Version®. Copyright © 1982 by Thomas Nelson. Used by permission. All rights reserved.

Scripture taken from the New Century Version®. Copyright © 2005 by Thomas Nelson. Used by permission. All rights reserved.

Scripture quotations marked ESV˙ are from the ESV Bible (The Holy Bible, English Standard Version˙), copyright © 2001 by Crossway, a publishing ministry of Good News Publishers. Used by permission. All rights reserved.

Scripture quotations taken from the Amplified® Bible, Copyright © 1954, 1958, 1962, 1964, 1965, 1987 by The Lockman Foundation Used by permission." (www.Lockman.org)

Cover and Page Layout Design: Josh Ezzell | Ezzell Creative
Copy Editor: Cally Ezzell

ISBN: 978-1-48356-557-6 (Print)
ISBN: 978-1-48356-558-3 (eBook)

Printed in the United States of America
A Faith Builders International Production
www.faithbuildersintl.com

Dedication

This book is dedicated in loving memory of my son, Gavin. I along with your mother, brother, and sister miss you everyday. Thank you son, for serving, and loving our family the way you did. Your example has shown me what it means to selflessly serve others, and it has also inspired me to write this book. Your life motivates us, and many others to live out our faith daily.

CONTENTS

Still in the Storm

FOREWORD

Growing up in Mississippi, I was in awe of southern thunderstorms. The winds would blow through the neighborhood, knocking down weak branches in the pecan trees and kicking up pine needles and leaves to let us know the storm had arrived. Then the rain would unleash a waterfall from the sky that would beat down the flowers and the plants in the yards and gardens. But what I remember most was the thunder. Brilliant flashes of lightning followed by earsplitting cracks of thunder always startled my mom and made her jump. I loved the storms, and I loved the thunder. We could hear a storm from miles away. I remember sitting on the front porch with my dad when we knew a storm was approaching, watching for lightning and counting the seconds before the thunder rumbled, so we would know how far away the storm was. Today, I could simply look up the radar on my cell phone and see the precise location of the storm, but technology will never take the place of those nights, sitting quietly with my dad, counting down the advance of the storm.

Looking back, I know that much of my love of storms was because I had no concern or anxiety. I was safe. I was in a sturdy home with a solid roof. I had no fear of the water rising too high or the winds blowing too hard. But mostly, I was not alarmed by the savage display of the elements because my dad was right there beside me. I was safe with my father.

As an adult, weather related storms still fascinate me, but life storms have brought a completely different level of awareness. Like weather storms, many times life storms are generated by circumstances beyond our control, and we are buffeted by circumstances and drenched in tears. Lightning strikes without warning and the thunderous effects leave us reeling. As the son of a pastor, and later as a pastor myself, I have been closely involved in numerous situations of both trial and tragedy. And I have learned a few things from these experiences that seem to mesh my Mississippi childhood with my knowledge as an adult. I know you can't stop a storm. I know you need to be protected. I know that the people around me help sustain me. And I know that my security is in my Father.

The character of a person is revealed without any obscurity or pretense during a life rocking storm. People are their truest selves when the unexpected happens, and they often act with notable grace and strength that is remembered for a lifetime. This is the case with my faithful friend, Jamey Santo. He has experienced severe life storms. His world has been altered in such a way that he can never go back. He has been ripped apart by situations that he could not control, and has been saturated with a downpour that continues to shape him every day. And throughout, Jamey has stood with strength, courage, conviction and trust.

The message Jamey Santo will share with you in this book, *Still in the Storm*, is made of truths that can only be fully understood through severe trials. His faith is more than words or ideas; it is the conviction of a man who has lived in the storm and is battle tested. Better than anyone I know, Jamey can personally share the truth that the only place of survival in a storm is in the presence of the Father.

I am privileged to have Jamey in my life and honored to be his friend.

Dr. Dave Martin
Success coach, inspirational speaker, and author of *Another Shot*

INTRODUCTION

I am very thankful you have decided to purchase this book at this time in your life. This book was written to help build your faith, no matter what season in life you may be in. You may be in a great season, or may find yourself in one of the hardest times you have ever faced. "Still In The Storm" is a book that was birthed out of the greatest tragedy of my personal and spiritual life. I wrote this book with you in mind, knowing that you or perhaps someone you know is facing a crisis, or one of life's biggest disappointments. It is my desire to be real and authentic with you while taking you on a journey that has its ups and downs but ends in victory.

I take you on a journey of faith not to inspire you, but to help you draw closer to God. Inspiration alone does not release everlasting change. It is through the revelation of God's word that you will see transformation take place within your own heart. I believe as you seek God with fresh faith through life's disappointments, you will discover powerful biblical truths that bring revelation. I am telling you when the revelation of God's Word is received by faith, that's when transformation happens from the inside out, not the outside in.

In this book you will discover three parts. Faith as our foundation. Faith as our freedom. Faith as our lifestyle. In each part contains chapters filled with powerful biblical truths that empower you to excel in every area of life, whether you feel like the waves are crashing in on you or whether you are sailing on calm seas. Whether you are on the mountaintop or the lowest valley. I encourage you to not let this become a book that just collects dust on a shelf or lays dormant in your E-reader. There is an interactive section at the end of each chapter, to help you reflect on what you have just read. First you will discover questions to help spur you on to think and grow. Secondly, you will discover a unique prayer for the specific topic you have just read. Lastly, you will discover some action steps that you can consider doing to put your faith into action.

The Lord spoke to my heart about launching the ministry of Faith Builders International a couple weeks after the greatest tragedy of my life. I will share this story with you in Chapter 1. However, it was many years ago that I had a strong impression in my heart to help build faith, restore hope, and extend God's love everywhere. I didn't have the blueprints on exactly what that would look like. I did know however, that one day authoring would be a part of His vision to help build faith through the revelation of His Word. The vision statement of Faith Builders International is to "Build Faith, Restore Hope, and Extend Love". Faith is the foundation that we build our spiritual lives on after we accept Christ into our lives. Faith in God allows you to experience freedom in many areas of life that the devil tries to keep you bound in. Faith is also a lifestyle that Christ invites us to live by everyday. You will discover that Faith is the fuel in the vehicle of Hope that takes you from where you are in life to where you want to be. Faith will help you reach your destination despite moments of disappointments and disturbances that life has brought your way.

As you turn these pages I believe your faith will be built, hope will be restored, and you will experience the tangibility of God's love.

PART ONE:
FAITH AS OUR FOUNDATION

CHAPTER ONE: STILL IN THE STORM

"And he arose, and rebuked the wind, and said unto the sea, 'Peace, be still.' And the wind ceased, and there was a great calm."

- Mark 4:39, King James Version

APRIL 1, 2015 –

I'm standing by the couch in our living room, my little boy's favorite spot in our house. I can picture Gavin running into this room and bounding onto it, eyes sparkling, to tell me about his day. I can see him sprawled across it watching our favorite teams play basketball on TV. Now, my eyes streaming, shoulders heaving, I stare silently down at Gavin's small, unmoving figure lying on it. I stroke the back of the soft hand I hold tightly in mine. Soon, funeral home attendants will knock on our front door. They will come inside, intent on taking my eight-year-old son from our home. Forever.

I'm not ready yet. I'll never be ready.

These are the last moments this side of Heaven I will ever spend with my fun maker.

My precious boy.

My miracle.

My Gavin.

How I wish this was some April Fools' joke. But it's not.

Peace, be still. The familiar voice echoes firmly, reassuringly, down to the very depths of my agonized soul.

I love you, God, but how can you say that to me right now? I'm your faithful follower. So is my wife Jeannie. We serve you every day. We have faith. We pray expectantly. We have people all over the world praying. We know you are a God of miracles. Where is our miracle now? I don't understand. I want Gavin back, Lord!

Inside, I scream.

You can raise him from the dead, God! Think of what a testimony that would be. I believe in you, Lord. I know you can do this. I have faith. I do.

And. I. Want. Gavin. HERE!

For a few seconds, there is only silence. Then the whisper comes again. *Peace, be still.*

I am right smack-dab in the middle of a raging storm of emotions – confusion, heartbreak, frustration, grief ... but somehow, I become still. I look down at my son's hand in mine. It does not move. I groan in anguish. Slowly, I uncurl my fingers and lay the small hand gently, oh-so-gently, down.

When my sorrows like sea billows roll,
it is well...
it is well...
with my soul.

* * *

In November, 2014, my middle child Gavin was diagnosed with an aggressive, stage four brain tumor. Out of the blue, our family of five was handed Gavin's death sentence. Until the month before, he had been a perfectly normal, fun-loving, basketball-playing eight-year-old boy. First came a few headaches, and one day my wife noticed Gavin's right eye turning in. Something just didn't seem right. So the day before Thanksgiving, off to the hospital we went. We had no idea this trip would change our lives forever.

At the hospital, doctors ordered an MRI. I suspected Gavin was just having migraines, but the MRI revealed much more. After the test was administered, doctors ushered me into a private room. Instantly, I knew something was very wrong. Six or seven medical professionals gravely delivered the devastating news. Gavin had a tumor in the back left side of his brain. They needed to perform a biopsy to see what kind of tumor we were dealing with.

I could not believe what I was hearing. This new reality slammed into me with the force of a freight train. I almost doubled over. How would I tell my wife? What would we tell Gavin and our other two kids? How would we make it through this? After the doctors gave me the news, I remember going back into the room with Gavin. I looked at my little boy, and in my heart I whispered to God, "I trust you even though I don't understand."

The following Tuesday, Gavin was taken into surgery for the biopsy to identify the type of tumor growing inside his head. Pathology put a rush on it and soon confirmed *glioblastoma multiforme*, a rare brain tumor that is one of the fastest-growing cancers in human beings. Prognosis? Grim. We had exactly one week from that first trip to the hospital until the diagnosis that told us we were in a race to try to save Gavin's life. A race the medical community assured us there was little hope of winning.

As the dad and leader of our family, naturally I want to fix things for everyone I love. As a minister, I am wired to help those in pain and need. I wanted to begin our offense. Pronto. Where do we start? How would we attack this nasty tumor, this evil growth trying to steal our son from us? If surgery to remove it was not an option, what was our battle plan? Jeannie and I tried to remain calm, but our emotions were going crazy.

We laid out our strategy medically and spiritually. With the doctors, we formulated a plan to start radiation. With our friends, family, church, and social media community, we asked people to pray. Jeannie and I went to the Lord continuously as well. We asked God to stop the tumor in its tracks. To reverse its course. To take it all away. We proclaimed our faith. We told the devil he had no right to come anywhere near our son. We anointed Gavin with oil. We believed God could and would heal Gavin. Someday, he would testify to the power of God that saved his life.

But just a few days after the biopsy results came back, Gavin began vomiting. I knew this was not a good sign. It could mean pressure was building in his brain. After being sick in the bathroom, Gavin became unresponsive. I noticed his right cheek moving up and down involuntarily. He began having a seizure. We dialed 9-1-1, and paramedics came and administered anti-seizure medicine. They loaded Gavin onto a stretcher, and back to the hospital we went. Suddenly, I was gripped by fear. I thought, *I don't know if I am going to make it through this. I could lose my son, right now. Oh, God, help us!*

Jeannie and I reached out to our dear friends to pray on Gavin's behalf, and I stayed by his bedside adding my own pleas. All through the night, doctors and nurses checked Gavin's responses. Sometimes his pupils retracted. Sometimes they didn't. Occasionally, he moaned. We called the nurse in two or three times to ask why he was not coming around. Finally, a doctor came in and looked at Gavin's brain scans. Then he looked at Gavin and ordered our son be taken to ICU immediately. He said the pressure in Gavin's brain from fluid buildup had to be alleviated.

Gavin was put into a medically induced coma to allow his brain to rest. An external shunt was inserted to relieve the pressure. Doctors said Gavin's seizure was a "pre-death" event. The rapidly growing tumor had caused the brain to shift. This, in turn, caused it to swell. When the brain swells too much, death occurs.

It was unbelievable.

Two weeks before, we were playing basketball in the driveway. Now, doctors told us to be prepared for our son to die.

On a Thursday morning in early December while Gavin lay in the induced coma, his doctor scheduled him for a procedure to insert an internal shunt. The shunt would drain excess fluid from his brain into his stomach. The doctor looked me in the eyes and told me she did not know if it would work. It was a risky procedure for anyone in Gavin's condition, and the outcome was far from certain.

Rallying my faith, I held her gaze and said, "We are *not* giving up on my son. He is not dying here. Not today. He is going to leave this hospital. I know my son, and I know how strong he is. He is going to come out of this."

Gavin made it through the procedure, and the next couple of weeks were touch-and-go. Gavin's brain was "resting" so he could recover from what doctors now believed was a stroke that occurred after the seizure he had at home. Resting might allow his brain to recover from the seizure and stroke, but every day of rest meant no treatment for the tumor. The tumor was still growing. Fighting the tumor with radiation might slow the tumor, but it also might overtax his injured brain. It looked like Gavin was losing the battle.

We invited family to come see Gavin one more time. My in-laws flew in, and everyone tried to prepare for the worst. However, I was still convinced Gavin was not leaving us yet. One night after everyone was gone from the hospital, I prayed, "Lord, I release Gavin to you. But please, help me get him home. He cannot die here. Help me get him home so we can have some time with him. So we can have Christmas together."

Gavin pulled through. The doctors took him off the ventilator and weaned him off the medications in hopes that he would wake up. He did, but the stroke left him severely weakened on his right side. We brought our precious boy home, now in a wheelchair, unable to talk like he used to. But still very much our fun maker. Our hilarious, sparkling Gavin. His sweet spirit still shined through.

Joy laced itself with sorrow as we celebrated the birth of our Savior. We had presents and a tree but Gavin was unable to participate as he laid in our bedroom, in his hospital bed, sleeping. We tried to capture as many moments together as we possibly could. We never lost hope that we would always be a family of five. After all, Gavin was God's miracle to us. We thought we had lost him when he was born. God healed him completely then and we had had eight precious years together so far.

Three months and one week after Christmas, Gavin's life on this earth ended. Could our family's faith stand such a test? How would we weather this storm?

* * *

I want to tell you right upfront that even though I did not see the results I wanted from my prayers for Gavin's physical healing, I never lost hope that the God I love was moving and working behind the scenes. Not once. My wife Jeannie and I had questions. We still do today. We wanted a different outcome. We still do today. We longed for a miracle here on earth with all our hearts. But our faith before, during, and after Gavin's diagnosis and death never, ever wavered. When my spirit cried out, "It is well with my soul," just after Gavin passed, I meant it.

Just as much as the author of that famous hymn did. "It Is Well with My Soul" was written by a wealthy Chicago lawyer who lived in the late 1800s. His name was Horatio Spafford, and he and his wife Anna had four daughters and a son. At the height of his professional success, in a very short span Spafford lost nearly everything he had. First, his young son died. Then, the Great Chicago Fire in 1871 wiped out his real estate investments. By 1873, Spafford's fortunes had recovered somewhat and he decided to take his family on a boat trip to Europe. He sent his wife and daughters ahead so he could take care of some business before he joined them. Their ship went down, and all four of his daughters were lost at sea. Only his wife Anna survived.

Grieving deeply, the lawyer set sail to England to be with his wife. During the ship's passage, Spafford wrote the words to the now-famous hymn, including the line: "When sorrows like sea billows roll … it is well with my soul."

How could he – how could I – maintain our faith in the midst of such overwhelming pain? Perhaps more importantly now that you are reading this book, how can you? When you have lost what is most important to you – whether it is your child, your marriage, your health, your career, or anything else that rocks your world completely – how can you have faith that God is good? How can you keep the faith at all? I believe it is by getting to know the author and finisher of it.

Hebrews 12:1-2 tells us to:

"... lay aside every weight, and the sin which doth so easily beset us, and let us run with patience the race that is set before us, looking unto Jesus the author and finisher of our faith; who for the joy that was set before him endured the cross, despising the shame, and is set down at the right hand of the throne of God." (KJV)

What does this mean for us exactly? Let's look at these verses carefully. First, Hebrews 12:1 instructs us to "lay aside every weight" and our "sin." Laying aside means to let go of it, to surrender it. We have to hand it over to God. We can't hold tightly to our sin, our shame, our worries, our anguish, our sorrows, or our grief. We are commanded to "lay aside." When a sentence starts with a verb (in this case, "lay") if you remember from middle school English, it is an "imperative" sentence. Imperative sentences have an understood "You" as their subject. So this verse really says: "(You) lay aside every weight ..."

Next, it tells us to "run with patience the race that is set before us ..." If you need to run with patience, you are not sprinting. The finish line is not a few hundred yards away. Races that require patience are marathons. They take a long time. They require a lot of endurance, and a lot of practice. You have to stay the course. I believe this tells us there are many things in our lives that will feel hard, terribly hard, but we have to keep putting one foot in front of the other. We can't always see where the course will lead us, what twists and turns it will take, but we must keep going if we want to finish. If we want to win.

You also run a marathon with an end goal in mind. The next part of this verse says, "looking unto Jesus." When we fix our focus on Him as our end goal, we are running in the right direction. He illuminates the path and gives us strength for the journey. As the "author and finisher" of our faith,

Christ both plants faith in us (authors it) and keeps it going no matter what (finishes it) … as long as we look to Him.

Finally, the rest of verse two tells us how and why Jesus endured the humiliating, torturous death on the cross … because of the "joy that was set before him …" meaning the suffering was worth it for the payoff. What is the payoff? It is our present reality that Jesus eradicated sin, and we are declared the righteousness of God in Christ Jesus. Our position is that we get to stand before God without a sense of guilt or inferiority. Because of our right standing in Christ, we can let faith shine in our hearts like the morning sun, resisting the fear the devil will try to plant in our hearts. Jesus position now is sitting at the right hand of God the father, praying for you and I. That is good news, even when dealing with bad news.

One key element of faith is to remember that we are infinite beings living in finite bodies in a finite world. In fact, we live in broken, finite bodies in a broken, finite world. We no longer dwell in the Garden of Eden. Nothing on this earth is perfect. However, because this earth is all we know, it can feel like this is all there is. Death feels final. But if you have a personal relationship with Jesus, death is not final. It never has the final victory. It is just a checkpoint in the marathon of life. The real finish line is Heaven. In eight short years, Gavin made it across the finish line of his life. He achieved victory.

"Then, when our dying bodies have been transformed into bodies that will never die, this Scripture will be fulfilled: 'Death is swallowed up in victory. O death, where is your victory? O death, where is your sting?'" (1 Corinthians 15:54-55, New Living Translation)

Frankly, death still stings for those left here on earth. It stings because our souls recognize death is not God's original plan for His kids. It separates us from each other. Death also separates those who do not believe in God from Him.

God created us as His precious children to spend eternity with Him in paradise beyond our richest imaginings. And that's part of the problem:

it is beyond our richest imaginings. That's where faith comes in. Faith becomes the bridge between finite and infinite.

Faith becomes the bridge between finite and infinite.

It allows us to have hope when it looks like hope is gone. It allows us to move forward when we would rather stop running, curl up, and give up.

1 Corinthians 13:12 puts it this way:

"For now we see only a reflection as in a mirror; then we shall see face to face. Now I know in part; then I shall know fully, even as I am fully known." (New International Version)

Let's unpack that too. In our finite time on earth, we only see a reflection of what life is truly like. When we die, we will be able to see all we were missing. We will know more. We will understand more. Until then, faith gives us the ability to move our lives forward. It covers us with peace in the most difficult situations. We can trust that a God who loves us enough to send His own son to die for our sins must see a bigger picture than we see.

Was Gavin healed in this life? No. Did he get off our couch and out of his wheelchair to play basketball again with his brother like he used to? No. Does that hurt me? Every single day. Do I want him here with us? Absolutely.

But, and here's the real test: Do I have faith that God is still God? One hundred percent and then some.

How about you? Do you have faith in Jesus, the author and finisher? Have you lost so much you can hardly breathe? Do you feel stuck, and hopeless? Have you become angry because it feels like God betrayed you? I mentioned a couple of times that Gavin was our miracle. I'll tell you all about that in upcoming chapters. Suddenly, Gavin was gone after eight short years.

Keep turning the pages and come with me on a journey of faith. A journey to renewed hope. A journey to unspeakable love. And plans to give you a hope and a future. (See this promise in Jeremiah 29:11.)

As my story unfolds, I pray yours will too. I pray that in the middle of your raging seas, your blackest storms, your darkest nights of the soul, you will be able hear, *Peace, be still.*

And you will be able to respond: *It is well with my soul.*

Still in the Storm: The First Steps

1. What storm are you standing in the middle of?

    _____

    _____

    _____

    _____

    _____

    _____

2. Where do you think God is in relation to what you are going through? What can you see Him doing in your life? (It's okay to say "nothing" if that's how you feel.)

    _____

    _____

    _____

    _____

    _____

    _____

3. What do you understand about faith and our lives on earth after reading Hebrews 12:1-2 and I Corinthians 13:12?

    _____

    _____

    _____

    _____

    _____

    _____

Still in the Storm: A Prayer for Faith

Dear Jesus,

I have to admit, I do not understand the storm I am in right now. I know there will be times when I may not understand, however, I come to you in Faith believing that all things are working together for my good because I love you. I thank you that I am invited into a life of faith, where I trust you even when I can't see the next steps ahead or fully understand what is going on. I thank you that when I feel like I am losing, you have already declared me a winner. Help me Holy Spirit to fully understand the revelation of the scriptures that God is for me and has never been against me. I thank you that you are close and never distant from me. Teach me to rely and depend on you despite of my natural senses. Thank you for building my faith today, and for helping me realize that I am declared the righteousness of God in Christ Jesus.

In Jesus's name,
Amen

Still in the Storm: The Next Steps

- Choose three to five Scriptures from this chapter and read them in different translations of the Bible. (Bible Gateway, www.biblegateway.com, is one website that makes this easy to do.) Which translations resonate with you? How did reading several versions of the verses give you better insight into what God is saying to you through them?

- Choose three verses and write them on sticky notes or three-by-five cards. Tape these to your bathroom mirror, place them on a bedside table, or hang them around your room. Make them as visible as possible, so you can read them multiple times daily. Say them out loud.

- Listen to the hymn "It Is Well with My Soul." Think about the words in light of the story you now know. What do Spafford's lyrics say to you now?

CHAPTER TWO: FEAR VS. FAITH

"The disciples went and woke him up, shouting, 'Lord, save us! We're going to drown!' Jesus responded, 'Why are you afraid? You have so little faith!'"

– Matthew 8:25-26(a), NLT

During Jesus's three years of ministry on earth, He picked twelve men to be His closest friends and followers. They became His disciples, and they traveled with Jesus a lot. Everywhere they went, Jesus taught and told stories. He performed miracles. He healed sick bodies, and cast out demons. He transformed small amounts of food into enough to feed thousands. He turned water into wine. He brought dead people back to life. Crowds followed Him wherever He went, often by the thousands.

His disciples witnessed it all. Again and again, they had front-row seats to watch the impossible happen with just a touch or a word from Jesus.

Three of the four gospel writers (Matthew, Mark, and Luke) tell the same story about Jesus and the disciples facing a storm. Jesus had been teaching all day, and so many people came to hear from Him that He taught from a boat near the edge of the sea. This way, the throngs could not crush Him. As evening came, Jesus told the disciples it was time to go to the other side of the sea. They set sail, and Jesus fell asleep in the stern of the boat. We can assume that he would have been exhausted from a full day of teaching. Suddenly, a huge storm came. The wind blew like crazy, and the waves came crashing into the boat. It began to fill with water, and the disciples started bailing. They began to panic. Meanwhile, Jesus kept sleeping.

As the waves broke over the bow, and the black clouds swirled overhead, the disciples woke Jesus. He sat up and simply said to his disciples, why are you afraid? Then He stated they had such little faith. It was obvious Jesus was not concerned about the stormey situation like His disciples were. Jesus then got up and told the wind and waves to be still. Instantly, the storm ceased.

I wonder if Jesus said it angrily or if He just looked puzzled. I wonder if the disciples made Him weary because of how little they understood even after all they had seen. I wonder if He was frustrated by their inability to hold onto their belief in Him under pressure.

I want to think that I would not have been afraid of that storm. I want to believe if I had seen all those miracles, I would have let that storm rage and taken a nap too. I try to convince myself if I had been a disciple, directly soaking up all the wise things Jesus taught and watching every miracle he performed, I would have spoken and calmed the storm myself. That way, I wouldn't have disturbed His rest.

Or would I have panicked just like the disciples did?

Before Gavin's death, I can tell you my answer might have been different than it is now. Proclaiming faith is one thing. Practicing it when you feel like you are drowning is something different altogether.

* * *

Gavin's death could have propelled Jeannie and I into a huge crisis of our faith. As the tumor attacked my little boy's brain, I felt like a small boy myself, standing alone in a boat with hurricane-force winds blowing, clouds as black as night racing overhead, lightning shooting through the sky all around me, and giant waves breaking over the bow. With every rock and tip of my small craft, I should have been plunged into the raging sea. I should have drowned in my own sorrow and helplessness.

Instead, I believed that the anchor – the hope I have through my faith in Jesus Christ – would hold. I stood firm in the boat, toes gripping for purchase, determined with everything in me not to go down. The devil might have the ability to make trouble. He might come to steal, kill, and destroy. But he was not going to get it all. I would hold on with all my might.

Before Gavin got sick, the condition of our family's life was pretty good. It was fairly smooth sailing. Fluffy clouds drifted overhead. Calm waters surrounded our boat. It was safe to travel. All of a sudden, the cancer storm struck.

Have you faced anything like that in life? Everything seems to be clear sailing, then – *BAM!* – a fierce storm strikes out of nowhere. One minute, everything is going great. Suddenly, with a word or a phone call or a diagnosis, everything goes wrong.

You will be faced with sudden storms in life. We all will. It's guaranteed. Jesus told the disciples in John 16:33: "In this world you will have trouble" (NIV). That's pretty clear, and it doesn't sound very fun. But then He finishes the verse by reminding His followers: "But take heart! I have overcome the world."

This indicates there must be two ways you can respond to the storms, crises, and trouble of all kinds that will come in this life. You can *respond* and "take heart" with faith. Or you can *react*, like the disciples in the storm, with fear.

You can choose to panic. You can let worry overtake you. You can let fear overcome you. Shoulders tensing. Heart pounding. Breath catching. Mind numbing. Fear closing in like waves crashing over you.

Or you can trust the One in the boat with you. The One who anchors you with hope. The One who saved you. The One who says He has "overcome the world." You can wait with peace that you don't even understand until He calms the storm.

Did you know that the King James Version of the Bible says, "fear not" seventy-one times? It also says again and again that we are not to be afraid. Fear is a big issue for people. God is well aware of this, so He reminds us in His Word not once, not twice, but hundreds of times not to worry, be afraid, give in to fear, or have anxiety. Over and over the Bible instructs us to choose faith, not fear, because He is with us. Here are three of those verses:

"Fear not, for I am with you; be not dismayed, for I am your God; I will strengthen you, I will help you, I will uphold you with my righteous right hand." (Isaiah 41:10, English Standard Version)

"Remember that I commanded you to be strong and brave. Don't be afraid, because the Lord your God will be with you everywhere you go." (Joshua 1:9, New Century Version)

"Even when walking through the dark valley of death I will not be afraid, for you are close beside me, guarding, guiding all the way." (Psalm 23:4, The Living Bible)

In the middle of life's storms, you can choose fear or faith. But you can't choose both. Fear and faith are opposites. They are enemies of each other. When fear takes residence in your heart, it reduces faith. On the flip side, strong faith trounces fear every time.

Because we are broken people living in a fallen world, fear feels more natural than faith. It tends to be our first response. When the paramedics loaded Gavin onto that stretcher after his seizure in our home, my immediate reaction was fear. I felt almost paralyzed with fear until I remembered to cry out to the One who is always with me. When I looked to Him, He calmed my storm. Not the external storm of my crisis, but the whirling, swirling storm of emotions inside me that were threatening to capsize me.

He whispered, "Peace, be still" to my spirit. And hope welled to the surface once again.

If Jesus is in your boat, you never have to be afraid. You can be assured of this because 1 John 4:18 says, "Such love has no fear, because perfect love expels all fear." From this verse, we know that love makes fear run for the hills. And what, or rather who, does the Bible say is love? Well, the same chapter of 1 John also says, "And so we know and rely on the love God has for us. God is love" (1 John 4:16(a), NIV).

God is love and love casts out fear. When fear leaves, peace enters. Storms calm. Faith engages. Circumstances may not change, but our ability to feel God's presence, to trust that He is working all things together for our good (Romans 8:28), increases astronomically.

When the disciples woke Jesus in the boat, He wasn't disturbed that they interrupted his nap. He was saddened that the disciples had chosen fear over faith in Him. His statement about having little faith was a reminder of all they had seen, heard, and experienced of the supernatural. Christ was basically saying, "Look, guys, you've seen the miracles. You saw me heal the man with leprosy. You were there when I healed Peter's mother-in-law. You know I cast out evil spirits with a simple command. Don't you get it by now that, awake or asleep, I can protect you through this storm?"

Your greatest suffering in life can turn into your greatest success if you can get rid of your fear and exercise faith instead. That's what Joseph did. In Genesis 37, Joseph's big brothers threw the teenage Joseph into a well, then sold him for twenty pieces of silver to some traveling traders. The brothers were jealous of Joseph because their father Jacob loved Joseph the most of all his sons. Their hatred for Joseph only increased after Joseph told them about a dream he had. In the dream, his brothers bowed down to him. The older brothers found Joseph's pronouncement ridiculous. They would never bow down to their baby brother. Instead, they vowed to get rid of him. After selling him to the traders, they smeared goat's blood on Joseph's coat and brought it to their dad to lead him to believe that a wild animal must have killed his favorite son.

The Bible spends nearly all of the rest of the book of Genesis telling Joseph's story. Joseph ended up in Egypt, and eventually found favor with the Pharaoh. Pharaoh came to rely on Joseph as his right-hand man. Years later when famine struck, Joseph's brothers came to Egypt trying to find food for their family so they would not die. Joseph recognized them right away. He ended up forgiving his brothers and saving his whole family from starving to death.

When Joseph's brothers plotted to eliminate him, Joseph could have been afraid. He could have allowed his fear to make him angry, resentful, and bitter. That resentment easily could have turned into revenge when his brothers turned up on his Egyptian doorstep needing food. Joseph could have paid them back by sending them away. Instead, he exercised faith by trusting that God was watching out for him all along.

In Genesis 50:20 (NIV), Joseph says, "You intended to harm me, but God intended it for good to accomplish what is now being done, the saving of many lives." Joseph recognized that God was in his boat. When the fierce storm came and Joseph's brothers sold him into slavery, Joseph chose faith. Through Joseph's faith, many lives were saved. What the devil no doubt thought was going to put Joseph down, God actually transformed into Joseph's divine purpose.

Jesus will do the same for you. Hebrews 13:8 (NLT) says, "Jesus Christ is the same yesterday, today, and forever." What He did for Joseph, He is already doing for you. Even if it seems like the storm is still raging. With God, there is always hope that rises in the midst of despair and distress. When you can identify purpose from the place where you feel the greatest pain, you will experience the greatest gain in your life.

When you can identify purpose from the place where you feel the greatest pain, you will experience the greatest gain in your life.

When Joseph's brothers came knocking on his door seeking food, his greatest pain became his greatest gain as he became reunited with his family. He was able to see his beloved father Jacob again. Joseph's sons received blessings from their grandfather. Joseph got to practice faith and forgiveness.

Jesus saw purpose on the other side of His suffering on the cross. He didn't want to experience it. Although He was fully God, Christ was also fully man. He felt every one of the whip's lashes. He agonized when thorns pierced his brow. He suffered incredible pain and humiliation in that torturous death on the cross. But He stayed the course. On the cross He declared, "It is finished," and in death He achieved eternal life with God for all of us who accept Him. His greatest pain became His (and our) greatest gain.

* * *

I don't know all of God's purpose in my son Gavin's death. I believe the devil cut Gavin's life short. The evil blight of cancer stole my son's potential on this earth. But nothing can steal God's ability to turn that evil act into some kind of good. I may not be able to see it all yet, but I am already getting glimpses. Despite this terrible storm, my family remains still in the boat, heading for the other side of the lake. Jesus sits in the boat with us. He will guide us and guard us as we go through this valley. And I believe we will reach the other side.

No matter what crisis or trial you are currently facing, I believe you will too if you invite Christ to be with you in the middle of your storm.

After the storm the disciples faced with Jesus, Matthew 8:28 says simply: "When Jesus arrived on the other side of the lake..." I am so blessed every time I read that verse to see that the disciples made it across that sea. They remained intact after the storm.

I want to encourage you in every storm to grab hold of whatever faith you can muster. A tiny seed of it will do. Just grab hold of Jesus and don't let go. Your anchor will hold. Peace will replace fear. You will remain above the surface. The waters of despair cannot drown you. You are going to fulfill all God has for you. You will make it to the other side.

Still in the Storm: Choosing Faith Over Fear

1. Why do you think the disciples became so afraid when the storm came knowing Jesus was with them?

    _____

    _____

    _____

    _____

    _____

    _____

2. Name a time in life when you reacted out of fear. What was the outcome? What do you think would have happened if you responded with faith?

    _____

    _____

    _____

    _____

    _____

    _____

3. What are you facing now that you need faith to overcome? How will you try to practice faith instead of fear?

    _____

    _____

    _____

    _____

    _____

    _____

Still in the Storm: A Prayer to Replace Fear with Faith

Dear Father in Jesus Name,

I know you are in my boat. I know you are the hope that anchors me when the storm rages. Today, I choose to allow my faith to grow in you and declare that fear has no place in my life. I am so grateful that you are bringing purpose and peace to my life from a place of chaos. Help me trust that you are working, even when I cannot see through the storm. When fear tries to grip me I thank you that you never leave me nor give up on loving me. The boat is rocking and I feel more than a little seasick, but I will trust you, Jesus. I put my faith in you. I thank you that you are bringing me to the other side where there is dry land and calm seas again. I confess that Jesus is Lord over every area of my life and fear has no hold on me anymore.

In Jesus's mighty name,
Amen

Fear vs. Faith: The Next Steps

- Make a list of the negative aspects of fear, contrasted with the positive benefits of faith. Hang your "pros and cons" list where you can refer to it often.

- Find three Bible verses in which God tells you not to fear. Write them down in a journal or on sticky notes or three-by-five cards and add them to the collection where you can read them daily.

- If fear or doubt tries to creep into your heart or mind this week, practice taking the thoughts captive. That means you may not be able to keep them from coming in initially, but you don't have to let them stay and take root. The moment you recognize a feeling of fear or a thought that makes you anxious, speak to it directly. Tell the thought it has no right in your mind or heart, that you are relying on Christ's love and grace, and tell it to leave. You may feel strange at first, but you will be surprised at how effective this can be.

- If fear starts to paralyze you, put on some praise music. Chase the fears away with melodies of God's love and grace.

CHAPTER THREE: THE FIRST LEAP OF FAITH

"I have been crucified with Christ and I no longer live, but Christ lives in me. The life I now live in the body, I live by faith in the Son of God, who loved me and gave himself for me."

- Galatians 2:20, NIV

I wasn't born a spiritual Superman. I did not come into this world with a cape of faith flying. No man (or woman) does. In fact, some could say the odds were stacked against me ever developing faith and trust in anyone or anything.

When my mother found out she was pregnant with me, my father wanted her to have an abortion. My mom was diabetic, and a pregnancy could kill her. Doctors also advised her against continuing with her pregnancy. They told her I could die in utero or during delivery, and that laboring with me could kill her. My mother chose to have me anyway.

She and I survived, but my parents' marriage did not. When I was still a preschooler, my mom and dad split up. In one of my earliest memories, I am sitting in the living room and I can hear my parents talking at the table about getting a divorce. Shortly after, my father left, and I have not really had a relationship with him since. I remember my mom taking me to my dad's new house for the weekend a couple of times. Then the visits just stopped. As a boy, I'm sure there were times when I longed for my dad.

Maybe I wanted him to come pick me up, take me fishing, or spend time with me. That didn't happen.

To me, life without a dad was not unusual. In the neighborhoods I lived in with my mom, fatherlessness was the norm. Most of the kids I knew lived with their moms. Or their grandmothers. I thought, *Oh well, this is just life.* I didn't know anything else.

The only time I actually recall feeling abandoned and disappointed by my dad was over a pair of shoes. I was around ten years old, and I started a business mowing lawns. I worked really hard at it. I saved money to buy my dad a Father's Day present. I wanted him to have new shoes. I worked and mowed and saved for months. Finally, I had enough to buy those shiny new shoes. I was so proud. I called my dad and told him about the gift I bought for him. He seemed excited and said he would come by to get them. He never did. That drove the final nail into the coffin of our relationship.

Although my mother loved me well, my childhood was often a lonely time. The only child of a single mom, I got shuffled from babysitters to school to my grandma's so my mother could work three jobs to support us. That remained our routine for years. The only male influence in my life came from Mom's come-and-go boyfriends. Most of them were not particularly good influences. I remember one man had severe depression. There was not much stability in my young life.

To top it off, at the end of second grade, doctors diagnosed me with Legg-Calve-Perthes disease. This childhood disorder affects the top of the femur, which is the ball of the hip joint. The growth plate located there stops getting enough blood circulated to it, and the bone softens and disintegrates. This caused my left leg to grow longer than my right. It was very painful.

A doctor in Orlando suggested my mother admit me to the Harry-Anna Crippled Children's Hospital in Umatilla, Florida. Back then, the hospital housed children with crippling diseases and disorders for extended periods of time. In another one of the few memories I have of my father, my parents presented a united front and dropped me off at the hospital together. I remember my mother crying when she told me she was leaving me there. My father looked at her and told her to "shut up."

I lived in the crippled children's hospital off and on for nearly two years. I spent six months of the first year flat on my back in traction. I got to know every ceiling tile like old friends. Following the time in traction, I spent months in a cast with a bar between my legs, extending them awkwardly. Surgeons installed a plate and screws in my hip, and then I got to spend time in grueling rehab. My mom visited on the weekends when she could.

After the first round of surgery and rehab, the hospital discharged me for almost a year. I resumed normal kid activities, even playing soccer. Then it was back to the hospital for another surgery to take out the plate and screws. Then more rehab to see if the hip would hold. Towards the end of my second stay, I was permitted to go home from the hospital on weekends. Finally, I was able to resume "normal" life. Except that my life wasn't really normal. My hip and leg got better, but my family circumstances didn't.

When I was fourteen, my mother remarried. Her new husband was a restaurant inspector. He also inspected my mother's daily activities. Suspicious and paranoid, he performed his job in the mornings. In the afternoons, he followed my mother. Stalked her, really. He thought she was cheating on him. I remember washing his government-issued car one time and seeing a stack of manila envelopes inside on the seat. As a curious teen, I pulled one out and started reading the contents. The journal-like entries detailed how he suspected my mom was having an affair with a local optometrist. My stepdad would park across the street from the optometrist's office and watch through binoculars each afternoon to see what my mom was doing.

My new stepdad also began drinking and became violent and abusive when he was drunk. On three different occasions, if I had not walked in from baseball practice or other activities at just the right moment, I have no doubt my stepfather would have killed my mother by choking her in his jealous, drunken rages. One time, he went on a rampage and punched out all our front windows. When I came home, broken glass and blood covered the walls, floor, and furniture. It looked like a murder scene.

My mother put up with his bizarre, violent behavior for too long, even after my stepfather was jailed or placed under psychiatric evaluation multiple times for different offenses. My mother kept taking him back, and our home life remained in turmoil. We lived in a run-down community where drugs, gangs, and violence were the norm right outside our front door.

One day, my stepfather really flipped his lid. He took his .357 Magnum and shot up the guest bathroom. Not knowing he had the gun, I walked into the bathroom. My stepdad turned, pointing his weapon directly between my eyes. I stared straight down the barrel. I thought I was as good as dead. Slowly, I backpedaled. I figured, I'm going to back up slowly, then turn around and start running like I've never run before. If he hits me, he hits me. I don't know why, but my stepdad didn't shoot me. Just shot up the bathroom.

After that incident, my stepfather got his act together again for about six months. He moved us into a new house and tried to turn his life around. I hoped he could hold it together and provide for my mom. I was now almost eighteen, and I wasn't sure I could take care of myself, let alone provide for my mom. Unfortunately, it didn't last. When the violence began again shortly after I turned sixteen, I looked at my mother and told her she could choose my stepfather and his violence or she could escape his wrath and leave with me. "It's him or me, Mom," I said. "You have a choice. I'm leaving and you can stay or come with me."

While my stepdad was at work one day soon after, my mother and I packed our clothes and the few belongings he had not broken or destroyed. (He had slashed up all the furniture by then.) My mother and I moved into a condominium and started our lives all over again.

* * *

Given the circumstances and challenges that filled my growing-up years, I could have ended up in jail. Or dead. I could have become addicted to drugs or sold them to escape poverty. I could have joined a gang. At the very least, I probably should have become bitter and resentful, sure that God and the whole world were against me.

Instead, only my self-esteem took a beating. The rest of my life remained fairly on track. Looking back, I think that's because I can see where God allowed points of His light to shine into the darkness of my circumstances. At different times when I was a kid, my mom sent me on the local church bus to vacation Bible school programs at the nearby Baptist church. Brother Bob picked us up and taught us about Jesus. I liked the stories, the crafts, and the snacks. It felt good to be there at the First Baptist Church of Pine Hills. My spirit stirred as I heard God's Word for the first time.

As a teenager, sports helped keep me on the straight and narrow. I played baseball. I played soccer. And I had a real knack for basketball. Playing ball provided me with mentorship and affirmation from the men who were my coaches. Sports helped me respect authority and taught me to be a member of a team. Athletics gave me a sense of being part of some-thing bigger than myself. I had to be accountable and take responsibility, give my best effort without always getting individual credit. It also afforded me the thrill of succeeding at something I worked hard at. Sports bol-stered my self-esteem and gave me something to look forward to. Practices and games kept me off the streets and provided me with a good reason to stay in school and try to keep my grades up. To this day, I love everything about hoops.

Even the bad experience my mother and I had with my stepfather turned out to have a silver lining. During the period when he moved us to our new home, we met neighbors who invited us to church. That invita-tion became the beginning of my personal relationship with Jesus Christ, a relationship that now means more to me than anything else in this world.

We attended Calvary Assembly of God in Winter Park, and I gave my heart to Jesus. I remember praying and asking Him to come in and take over my life. In that moment as I truly met God for the first time, I reflected back and started processing all of the feelings of abandonment I had stuffed down, all of the ways I had felt "less than" because of my past. I started crying and crying. I remember going down to the front of the church and giving all that hurt and shame to the Lord. I surrendered my will and my circumstances to Him.

Immediately, I remember this overwhelming cleansing feeling. I literally felt washed clean. I knew I was free from all the stuff in my past. I received freedom from any brokenness and pain. It was an amazing feeling. I knew then and there Jesus was real. I had a supernatural encounter with a God who was bigger than any wounds left by my dad, bigger than any scars my past tried to put on me, bigger than any blows to my self-esteem my circumstances tried to give me. I was healed from the hurts my dad, my hospitalizations, and my chaotic home life gave me. And it all happened in an instant. One moment, I knew of Jesus. The next moment, I knew Jesus as my personal Savior.

One moment, I knew of Jesus. The next moment, I knew Jesus as my personal Savior.

* * *

Where did my faith come from? How did I take that tiny-yet-transforming leap into the unknown realm of believing in Jesus Christ? Why can some people hear the gospel and ignore it, while others like me embrace it as truth? Let's take a look at where the Bible says faith comes from. We'll start in Romans 12:3. Here, the Apostle Paul is instructing Roman believers in Christ on how to act as His followers. Notice the phrase at the end of the verse.

> "For by the grace given me I say to every one of you: Do not think of yourself more highly than you ought, but rather think of yourself with sober judgment, *in accordance with the faith God has distributed to each of you.*" (NIV, italics added for emphasis.)

So this verse tells us God distributes faith to each one of us, but how? If you back up two chapters to Romans 10:14-17, Paul says the following:

> "How then shall they call on Him in whom they have not believed? And how shall they believe in Him of whom they have not heard? And how shall they hear without a preacher? And how shall they preach unless they are sent? As it is written: 'How beautiful are the feet of those who preach the gospel of peace, who bring glad tidings of good things!' But they have not all obeyed the gospel. For Isaiah says, 'Lord, who has believed our report?' So then faith comes by hearing, and hearing by the word of God. (NKJV)

According to Paul's epistle to the Romans, everyone gets a measure of faith from God. When do they get it? When they hear the word of God. Faith comes by hearing. Hearing means not only listening to the story of the gospel with your ears, but also listening with your heart and soul. The spark of faith ignites inside you when the gospel story starts to resonate within you.

The spark of faith ignites inside you when the gospel story starts to resonate within you.

You can choose to ignore what you heard, put out the spark, and your faith will not grow. Or you can grow hungry to hear more, and your faith can explode.

When I heard the Word of God, I wanted more of Him. It made sense to me. I was not just hungry; I was ravenous for His story. How could this Jesus, fully God, choose to leave the splendor and glory of Heaven and live a difficult life as a human being so he could understand my sufferings? How could He choose to die for my sin? No one had ever loved me like that, accepted me like that. In Jesus's eyes, I was a superhero. His son. To Him, I was a prince, a brother, an heir with Him to the kingdom of God. I had never been any of those things to anybody. I wanted to be seen like that. To be known like that. To be accepted like that by the God who created the entire universe. What a gift! For me it was a no-brainer. I had longed for that kind of acceptance all my life.

Jesus thought so much of me (and you) and loved us so much that He yielded His will to God and saw purpose beyond the excruciating pain he endured on the cross. We know this because in the gospels of Matthew, Mark, and Luke, Jesus has an intense conversation with God the Father right before he is betrayed and arrested. He knows He will soon be going to His death, and He is not looking forward to it. "Abba, Father," he cries out, "everything is possible for you. Please take this cup of suffering away from me. Yet I want your will to be done, not mine." (Mark 14:36, NLT)

"Abba" means "Daddy." Jesus is asking "Daddy" to save His life, while at the same time, and in the same breath willingly accepting what

He knows His dad wants Him to do. This is the prayer of consecration and dedication. Jesus yielded his will to God's will. We are worth that much to Him. Not just the pain He endured as a human being, the humiliation and torture. But death. The first and last time Jesus was separated from God. There was a break in communication, in relationship, when Jesus had to become our sin. He became cursed for us during that period of death. It was my sin, your sin, hanging on that cross. Our sin, our baggage, our hang-ups, our fear. All of that died on that cross that day. It was the day that everything changed.

Christ descended to hell to wrestle the keys of death away from Satan. And he emerged victorious when He rose from the dead and proved to the world that the love of God is stronger than anything evil can try to pull. It always has been. It always will be. To the end of time. No matter what happens. No matter what comes against us. If we are in Christ, we win. Period. End of story.

The moment Jesus overcame death, a covenant was established, rescuing us from the curse of sin that the law puts on us.

> "But Christ has rescued us from the curse pronounced by the law. When he was hung on the cross, he took upon himself the curse for our wrongdoing. For it is written in the Scriptures, 'Cursed is everyone who is hung on a tree.'" (Galatians 3:13, NLT)

When we become Christ followers, we now are found when before we were lost. We have freedom when we used to be bound. We can experience joy when we used to be sad. We can love when we used to be hateful. The cross allows people to go directly to God through the name of Jesus and have direct access to Him. In the Old Testament, the only one who had direct access to God was the high priest of the temple. And that was only once a year. The presence of God resided inside the Ark of the Covenant, which stayed behind a veil in the temple. The area was called the "Holy of Holies." Once a year, the high priest could go behind the veil in order to offer a blood sacrifice for his own sins and the sins of all the people. That's it.

Since Jesus died on the cross, took our sins upon Himself, and resurrected from the dead, people who accept Christ gain instant access to God. I think today we forget what an incredible, amazing thing this is. We can talk to God anytime we want to. We can enter His presence by praying and asking and seeking Him. His Spirit dwells inside us, rather than inside of a box made according to God's specifications and tucked behind a veil in a temple. In fact, when Jesus said on the cross, "It is finished," the earth literally quaked, the sun eclipsed, and the temple veil was supernaturally ripped in half from top to bottom. The distance between man and God was instantly erased. Does that give you goose bumps? It certainly gives them to me.

* * *

Once I realized the depth of Christ's sacrifice for me and accepted Jesus into my heart, I needed and wanted to grow my faith. I started to spend time in fellowship with other Christians at church. The administrator at the Church I attended Dave Taylor, took me under his wing. In my teenage years, I spent a lot of time at Dave's house. He was the first person to expose me to what a family is really all about. At the Taylor home, we all sat around the dinner table, eating and sharing about our day. I began to read my Bible and to pray more too. When my spirit "heard" the Word of God, my faith grew.

Over time, I started feeling a call to go into ministry. I got involved in the youth group playing drums and soon became a youth leader. While I helped with the youth, the experience I received with the youth group discipled me. I started working full time at a Christian Bookstore, and I volunteered another forty hours a week at the church. The lead pastor noticed my passion for ministry and encouraged me to attend Bible school. For two years, I attended Rhema Bible Training Center near Tulsa, Oklahoma. From 1995 to 1997, I studied, learned, and grew some more.

My faith spark fanned into flames while working with the youth. Now, as I studied at Rhema, it spread through me like wildfire. Why? Because I was hearing the Word, meditating on it night and day. Remember what we just read? "Faith comes by hearing, and hearing by the Word of God" (Romans 10:17). When you are constantly listening to God's Word, your measure of faith increases enormously.

Throughout my twenties and into my early thirties, I experienced a spiritual "honeymoon" as my relationship with the Lord deepened. I also met and married my beautiful, God-loving wife Jeannie. We dedicated our lives and marriage to the Lord, ministering at a church in central Florida. After several years of marriage, we started a family when our first son Preston was born on July 30, 2004.

For more than a decade after I took that first leap of faith in my teens, acting on what God had planted within me, I sailed along on glassy seas. Jeannie and I had the usual adjustments of job changes, moves, and other small waves breaking over our bow. But for the most part, life was sweet. Skies were blue, and nothing threatened my family's boat.

During our honeymoon period of faith, my wife Jeannie and I had no idea that just a couple of years later, the tides would turn against us. The biggest storm of our lives was just a few years over the horizon. Our faith felt strong on calm seas. But when the hurricane hit, we found our faith was strong enough to hold. Even as we felt battered and beaten, we remained in the boat. It did not capsize. Christ remained beside us, comforting us as our mouths filled with salt water and our eyes stung with tears. He continues to anchor us even now so that we do not drown.

Where do you stand in your faith today? Have you taken that first tiny-yet-transforming leap? Maybe you asked Jesus into your heart when you were a child, but the curveballs life has thrown at you caused your heart to drift away from Christ. Maybe you never believed in Jesus as your Savior but now realize He is in the boat with you in your storm and you are ready to allow His peace to enter into your soul. Maybe you experienced strong faith in Christ in the past, but it took a beating as the wind and waves of life pounded against you.

I strongly encourage you to ignite or relight the fire of your faith today. Right now. You will never regret it. God's Word states you already have a measure of faith within you. All you have to do is tend that spark. Ask Christ to be with you and He promises He will be. Forever. Faith can carry you through life's storms. In fact, from personal experience I am fully convinced it is the only way to keep your sanity in the midst of unimaginable, unexplainable tragedy. Aren't you ready for that today?

Still in the Storm: Igniting the First Spark of Faith

1. When did you take your first tiny leap of faith? Where were you? What happened? How did you feel?

   _____

   _____

   _____

   _____

   _____

   _____

2. What circumstances fanned that first faith spark into a flame? How have you nurtured your faith?

   _____

   _____

   _____

   _____

   _____

3. What, if anything, has kept you from igniting the spark of flame the Lord has placed within you? If you have never taken a tiny leap into faith, are you ready to now?

   _____

   _____

   _____

   _____

   _____

Still in the Storm: A Prayer to Ignite Faith

Dear Father In Jesus Name,

Thank you for being the author of my faith. Thank you for being the finisher of my faith. Thank you for your Word which promises you have given me a measure of faith. Today, I want to ask you to fan that spark of faith into a roaring flame. I believe in you. I believe you perform miracles, even when my circumstances do not show evidence of them. Even when it looks like the evil one is winning.

Come into my life right now, Jesus. I surrender everything to you. I recognize that you died on the cross for me and for my sin. I also recognize that you have risen from the grave and now I have freedom from my past so I can leap into the future you have for me. Please forgive me for all that I have done wrong. I invite you into my life right now. Clean out my heart and make me ready for the big things you have planned for me. I want you to reign in my life. I thank you that the Holy Spirit dwells in me and comforts me. I thank you as I take this leap of faith that you are with me and empowering me to succeed. I declare that you are my Lord and I receive everything you have for me by faith.

In Jesus's mighty name I pray,
Amen

The First Leap of Faith: The Next Steps

Author's note: First of all, if you prayed this prayer to ignite faith and it is the very first time you have ever asked Jesus to come into your heart and life, congratulations! You have become what the Bible calls, "born again," ready for a whole new life covered in the forgiveness of Christ. We are so excited for you. Even though your circumstances may not have changed in ways you can see in the last few minutes, your life for all eternity has changed completely. You are a child of God, and you can now be assured you will spend eternity with Him in Heaven. And you know what? I can't wait to spend it with you.

To grow in your newfound faith, it is important that you take a few next steps:

- Tell another believer in Christ that you have taken this step, and ask that person to help you take the next steps to grow.

- Find a solid, Bible-teaching church where you can grow in knowledge and wisdom, as well as spend time with others who have faith in Jesus.

- Get a good study Bible if you don't have one and begin reading God's Word every day. You will be amazed at the many ways this God-breathed book is completely relevant to your life today.

PART TWO: FAITH AS OUR FREEDOM

CHAPTER FOUR: FINDING IDENTITY

"But whoever is united with the Lord is one with him in spirit."

1 Corinthians 6:17(a)

Maybe because I grew up without knowing the love of a father, figuring out my identity was a struggle. As a teenage boy becoming a young man, I did not know who I was. I certainly did not understand *whose* I was. Faith can be hard to find when you don't know who you are or what your purpose is. Once you understand your true identity in Christ, faith becomes the easy part.

What do I mean by identity? Let me explain. "Identity," according to Merriam-Webster.com, means several things. It is 1. "the condition of being the same with something described or asserted"; 2. "who someone is: the name of a person"; 3. "the qualities, beliefs, etc., that make a particular person or group different from others."

When you compare those three definitions to what you receive from Christ when you accept Him and His work on the cross, the enormity of the gift should start to sink in. You become "the same" with Christ. As 1 Corinthians 6:17 says, you are "one with him in spirit." You take on His identity. Your identity is found in Him. Who Christ is becomes who you are. You bear His name. His likeness. His character qualities. His acceptance by God the Father. His status in Heaven and on earth. Wow! Think about that.

That means no matter what happens in your life, God never changes His mind about how He feels about you. Your attitude, your temperament (or temper), even your bad hair days do not change one iota of God's love for you and His full acceptance of you. Just like you are. On your worst days as well as your best.

Every human being struggles to figure out their identity and purpose. I believe it is one of the devil's biggest weapons against us. He tries to use every distraction and smokescreen he can to keep us from discovering our identity in Christ, as we ask life's biggest questions. Why are we here? What are we supposed to accomplish? How do we connect with other people? How can we become loved?

As human beings created in God's image, we long and strive for acceptance. We want to be recognized as special, loved unconditionally, and understood to the depths of our souls. All of these longings are fulfilled only by finding our true identity in Christ. Therefore, the devil tries to keep us from that by throwing distractions at us. Distractions like fatherlessness, busyness, money, television, duties, work, addictions, unhealthy relationships, low self-esteem, or anything else that will eat up our time, cause us to feel terrible about ourselves, or keep us from pursuing a relationship with God. Satan uses every sleight of hand to prevent us from figuring out our true, healthy identity in Christ.

Fame and fortune do not give us healthy identities, or every big-name actor and celebrity would be the happiest person on earth. Too often, we have seen how fame and fortune instead lead to addiction, depression, and self-destruction.

We can't work for our true identity either. Even if the work we are doing is for God. One mistake many Christ followers make is to get so excited about the miracle of salvation that they immediately begin working hard for God after asking Jesus into their hearts. They dive into volunteering at church, leading classes, making food, teaching Sunday school, running programs … anything to help build God's kingdom. Their motives are pure, but all too often the work begins to wear them down. They begin to focus more on duty than on their relationship with God.

When work replaces study, rest, communication with God, and real fellowship with others, we can become disillusioned in our faith. Burned out. Dried up. Unable to feel the joy of the Lord. We go from accepting the free gift of Christ to working ourselves to death to prove something to Him. We don't have to.

In the Bible, a woman named Martha learned that lesson directly from Jesus. Martha was a hard worker, the sister of Lazarus, a friend of Jesus. In fact, in the book of John we read that Lazarus got really sick and died, and Jesus brought him back from the dead. Martha witnessed this. No doubt she felt like she owed Jesus a lot. One time when Jesus came to Martha's house, she started bustling around, trying to get food ready and make the house hospitable for the Lord.

Martha's sister Mary didn't help Martha get ready. Instead, she sat down near Jesus and just listened to Him. Martha got annoyed with Mary. She couldn't believe she was left to do all the housework and meal preparation by herself. She complained to Jesus in Luke 10:38-42 (NIV):

"As Jesus and his disciples were on their way, he came to a village where a woman named Martha opened her home to him. She had a sister called Mary, who sat at the Lord's feet listening to what he said. But Martha was distracted by all the preparations that had to be made. She came to him and asked, 'Lord, don't you care that my sister has left me to do the work by myself? Tell her to help me!'

'Martha, Martha,' the Lord answered, 'you are worried and upset about many things, but few things are needed—or indeed only one. Mary has chosen what is better, and it will not be taken away from her.'"

What did Jesus mean? I think His message for Martha is the same today for us. That sitting at His feet is sometimes the most important thing we can do. Listening to His voice means more than work. Absorbing His presence does more for our relationship with Him than all our efforts to please Him. Our true identity is revealed when we simply get close to Christ.

We won't discover our true identities in our careers, our kids, our homes, our cars, our hobbies, or even our ministries. We can't work our way into an identity in Christ. We can't buy our way into it. What the devil knows and does not want us to figure out is that it is already ours. A free gift, if we will accept it. It's that easy to receive. And that is hard to wrap our minds around.

* * *

Once you catch even a glimpse of who your identity is in Christ, it becomes your defining moment – the greatest change in your life. Have you ever been in a pitch-black room where you can't see a single thing? You grip your cell phone in your hand, afraid to take a step forward for fear you will bash your shins, when you remember your flashlight app. You touch the screen in the dark and watch the beam of light suddenly illuminate the space in front of you. Now you can see your next step clearly. The dark has been banished and the room transformed by the light.

When you start to pore over the Bible verses that teach about what Jesus did on the cross, why He came to this earth, and how many wonderful promises He has for you in His Word, you begin to have light in your dark circumstances. You start to see what your next steps should be. You recognize that everything you worked for, tried to build on your own, the identity you created for yourself, means nothing compared to your true self in Christ.

Once you ignite the measure of faith God placed in you, you change from the inside out. Your situation often looks the same, yet you are not the same at all. You are in Christ. A new creation. Through His power and strength, you realize that God places His super on your natural. You have the supernatural power of God within you. Power to shed addictions. Power to eliminate self-esteem issues goodbye forever. Power to quite striving for acceptance. Power to rest in the knowledge that you are enough.

You always have been enough for the One who created you, who knew you before the beginning of time, who knit you together in your mother's womb. Psalm 139 is a wonderful chapter to memorize. Every one of its twenty-four verses speaks of how intimately God knows you and me.

> "O LORD, you have examined my heart and know everything about me. You know when I sit down or stand up. You know my thoughts even when I'm far away. You see me when I travel and when I rest at home. You know everything I do. You know what I am going to say even before I say it, LORD … You made all the delicate, inner parts of my body and knit me together in my mother's womb. You saw me before I was born … Every day of my life was recorded in your book. Every moment was laid out before a single day had passed. (Psalm 139:1-4, 13, 16 NLT)

Your true identity was issued once and for always by the living God. The God who recorded every day of your life in His book before you were born. The God who paid the price of His only son's life in order to reconcile you to Himself forever. In order that you might embrace your true identity in Him.

When you accept Jesus's sacrifice for you, you become a new creation. You receive His identity. Second Corinthians 5:17-18 states the following:

"This means that anyone who belongs to Christ has become a new person. The old life is gone; a new life has begun! And all of this is a gift from God, who brought us back to himself through Christ."

The life of who you were before Christ is not who you are with Christ right now. Isn't that great news? Galatians 4:6 reminds us that we actually have the Spirit of Christ in us, transforming us.

> "Because you are his sons, God sent the Spirit of his Son into our hearts, the Spirit who calls out, 'Abba, Father.'" (NIV)

We are His children, no longer a part of the old but rather a part of the new life God intends for us to live. And once inside our hearts, the Holy Spirit does the work for us if we allow him to do it. Look at how often Scriptures reassure us of our full acceptance in Christ.

> "Christ accepted you, so you should accept each other, which will bring glory to God." (Romans 15:7, NCV)

> "For in Christ all the fullness of the Deity lives in bodily form, and in Christ you have been brought to fullness. He is the head over every power and authority." (Colossians 2:9-10, NIV)

> "We know that our old sinful selves were crucified with Christ so that sin might lose its power in our lives. We are no longer slaves to sin." (Romans 6:6, NLT)

> "Since, then, you have been raised with Christ, set your hearts on things above, where Christ is, seated at the right hand of God. Set your minds on things above, not on earthly things. For you died, and your life is now hidden with Christ in God." (Colossians 3:1-3, NIV)

What is the true identity of a Christ follower? The identity of Christ. The fruit of the Holy Spirit. We can have love, joy, peace, patience, kindness, goodness, gentleness, faithfulness, and self-control. We can shed bad habits. We can love unconditionally. We can display the attributes of love that are found in 1 Corinthians 13. We no longer have to fall prey to Satan's traps. We can tell him to get lost every time he tries to trick or tempt us. We know this because the Bible tells us so.

Our identity is in Christ, and our position is with Him. Jesus Christ ascended to Heaven and currently sits on a throne at the right hand of God. Our position in Heaven is with Him. Our flesh may be here on earth for now, but our rightful place is in paradise with Christ.

My son Gavin is already there, experiencing the fullness of the joy of being with Christ for eternity. He didn't have to work for it or earn it. Some months before he died, Gavin asked Jesus into his heart. He accepted the work Christ did for his sin on the cross. And on April 1, 2015, God welcomed my boy into His presence in paradise. God knew the number of Gavin's days before he was formed in Jeannie's womb. And while I believe God despises all disease and destruction of the people He created in His image, He was not surprised by Gavin's appearance in Heaven. He was ready and waiting with open arms.

I still see through a mirror darkly, but Gavin's eyes are now opened. It is my faith that allows me to believe with everything in me that I will see my son again. We will be together for eternity with Jesus. What a glorious reunion that will be!

I know my ID was issued by God through the work His son Jesus did on the cross to make a covenant with me. My identity is found in Him all the time, no matter what situation or circumstance I find myself in. Everything around me may change, but who I am does not. *Whose* I am does not. I am a child of the King of Kings, heir to the throne, adopted son of God through Christ.

Are you finding your worth, your position, your acceptance in Christ and Christ alone? Or are you looking for validation from your wife, your boss, your children, your friends, or your parents? Only Jesus can truly fulfill you. Only His identity can truly satisfy your longings and show you your purpose.

Still in the Storm: Finding Identity

1. What are some of the ways outside of Christ that you have tried to discover your own identity?

    _____

    _____

    _____

    _____

    _____

    _____

2. What do you receive through Christ's work on the cross for you? How does it give you a new identity?

    _____

    _____

    _____

    _____

    _____

    _____

3. What are some things you can do to remember your identity in Christ when you find yourself slipping into old ways or when you face a tough situation?

    _____

    _____

    _____

    _____

    _____

    _____

Still in the Storm: A Prayer of Identity

Dear Father in Jesus Name,

First, I want to thank you for your Son Jesus that did an amazing work on the cross. Thank you Jesus for dying for my sin, so that I can discover my righteous identity in you. Thank you for giving me a true identity. A identity that is not found in this world but in Christ. I thank you that the Holy Spirit is helping me see clearly everyday that my identity is not found in what I do, what cars I drive, or what things I have accumulated. My identity is in Christ and His love for me. Help me to live out the identity you have given me. Holy Spirit, root out any areas of sin that could cloud my vision of Christ in me. I thank you that I am not "less than." I am good enough for Jesus. Thank you that I am accepted just as I am. As Christ is in me I declare that I have all sufficiency to succeed in every area of my life. I thank you Lord, that you are faithful to complete the work that you have started in my life.

In Jesus loving name I pray,
Amen

Finding Identity: The Next Steps

- Find a comfy, quiet spot and read the book of John in one sitting. Consider the life, teachings, and sacrifice of Jesus Christ. Thank the Lord for what He did on the cross to give you a new identity in Him.

- Do something creative that shows who you are as a new creature in Christ. Make a collage of images, draw a picture, or create a Pinterest board of sayings and images that show your new Identity.

- Read all four gospel accounts of Jesus's death. Then do some research about death on a cross. What did Jesus experience? What did dying on a cross symbolize to the Romans? Try to go deeper in understanding exactly what price Jesus paid for you to have eternal life. Rejoice in the fact that you are now made righteous because of the full price that Jesus paid for all of your sin.

CHAPTER FIVE: PEAKS AND VALLEYS

"Yea, though I walk through the valley of the shadow of death,

I will fear no evil;

For You are with me;"

Psalm 23:4 (NKJV)

On August 24, 2006, my son Gavin was born. And on August 24, 2006, my son Gavin died … the first time.

For Jeannie and me, it was our first experience walking in the valley of the shadow of death with the little family we were creating. Instead of joyous expressions on the doctor's and nurse's faces with the wonderful news "It's a boy!" followed by the healthy cries of a newborn entering the lights and sounds of the world for the first time, Gavin came into this world still and silent. Not a healthy, pink-hued baby at all, but a sickly grayish-blue. His medical chart for the first several minutes of life described his color as "dusky." Gavin made no effort to breathe. He had no heartbeat. Medical personnel hovered over his little body, working frantically on him from the moment he emerged. They had to resuscitate him.

Doctors said he lacked oxygen for too long during the birthing process. His Apgar scores were zero to two instead of a healthy nine or ten. When he was wheeled back to the nursery, he still wasn't moving at all. Even after he had been resuscitated and was breathing on his own, he was not responding like a new baby should. For three days, multiple doctors and specialists ran tests and examined Gavin. They weren't sure what was wrong. They told us he was having seizures. I wasn't sure we were getting all the information we needed. We thought Gavin had heart problems. Finally, Gavin was transported to a specialized children's hospital. There, a team of specialists, including a neonatologist and a neurologist, sat us down and told us the bad news.

Gavin was severely brain damaged because of a lack of oxygen, they said. He wasn't responsive even to needles pricking the bottoms of his feet. He could have cerebral palsy and a host of other developmental delays and issues. The list of conditions we were told Gavin could have went on and on. Jeannie and I sat there in shock. We thought the news might be bad, but nothing prepared us for this. Gavin was still twitching and jerking with seizures, and the doctors' opinions were that he would never be "normal." They were still going to run tests, including a spinal tap and brain MRIs, to determine exactly how bad Gavin's condition was and what, if anything, could be done.

Jeannie and I felt devastated. Driving home after hearing the news, I pulled the car over and we began to pray. I thought back to what I had learned from my Bible college days at Rhema. I recalled Pastor Kenneth Hagin's voice telling us in class that where the will of the Lord is, you will always have peace. I did not have peace right then, not after that terrible news. So I began to plead in prayer on my tiny son's behalf.

"Lord, I don't have peace about anything the doctors said, so I do not believe this is your will for Gavin. I believe, God, that you can and will reverse this so that there will be nothing wrong with our son's brain. I believe, Lord, you can restore him so he will develop perfectly normal."

Then I prayed specifically against the potential diagnoses the doctors had spoken over Gavin. I declared that he would not have cerebral palsy. Or multiple sclerosis. Or any of the diseases or disorders the doctors were predicting. Jeannie agreed with me in prayer. Right there in the car on our way home from the hospital, we waged war for our newborn son's health and life. I was determined to cancel the negative words of the doctors with our prayers.

The next day, we returned to the hospital and the doctors told us they were going to do an MRI on Gavin's brain, as well as an EEG to check his brain activity. They told us they expected to find that there was not much activity at all. They warned us they feared he might have little healthy brain tissue. That day, Gavin opened his eyes for the first time. We continued to pray. When the tests were done, the technician called the doctor and asked what it was he was supposed to be looking for. He reported that he was looking at a perfectly normal brain scan and was not sure what the doctor thought was wrong. The MRI and EEG were fine.

Gavin's doctor looked at me with an expression of shock that said he had no idea what had just happened. But Jeannie and I knew. We were witnessing a miracle. Satan was not going to take our baby boy from us. His days were recorded in God's book, and they were not over yet.

One of Gavin's doctors was so amazed that he would take our son around the unit and show him off to everybody in this office, exclaiming that he didn't know how this had happened. We knew the Lord had healed him. Over the first three months of his life, Gavin had to be monitored at home for seizure activity, and Jeannie spent many a night rocking him and watching over him. Then that stopped, too, and Gavin never had any major health issues again. He developed normally, and in fact was ahead of grade level in some areas when he entered school.

I feel very confident in saying the Lord provided a miracle to us. We definitely could see hand of the Lord in Gavin's life. He was a walking, talking miracle. Full of joy. Absolutely hilarious. He was outgoing. He was very orderly and detailed. He was incredibly smart. Like I've said, he loved basketball just like his daddy. He looked up to his big brother Preston. He almost always wore a big smile. He was our fun maker.

So when we got the news eight years after his traumatic birth and total healing that Gavin was almost certainly going to die from a *glioblastoma*, our faith could have taken a huge nosedive. Right then and there, we could have turned our backs on God. Felt like He betrayed us. Like He gave us a miracle and now it was being taking it away. What sense did that make? None at all. Not to us. Honestly, it still doesn't make sense. This is when you need faith the most. When things don't make sense, faith that keeps you close to God. Faith does not operate by feelings. Faith operates by love, and it is love that causes you to move forward when you feel like going backwards.

When Jeannie was pregnant with Gavin, she had an unprecedented supernatural experience. She was in the nursery praying over what was to be Gavin's room, when suddenly the room darkened. She felt like there was a strong demonic presence in the room and it scared her. Then she heard a voice in her spirit telling her that Gavin would never see that room. That we would never bring him home alive. She began to pray fervently, and what she felt so strongly that day did not come to pass. Gavin did come home to his nursery. He developed normally, and gave us eight years of adventure and joy.

Yet even while she was still pregnant, Jeannie sensed there was a supernatural battle going on over the life of our son Gavin. We will probably never know until we reach Heaven why Gavin only got to spend eight years on this earth with us. Still, and this is the point we hope you will grasp in this book, we trust God. We choose to rely on our faith. That God has a plan. That His ways are higher than our ways. God through His Holy Spirit is our Comforter and our Provider. He is yours also.

When the questions and doubts try to work their way into our thoughts, we quickly fall back on what we know about God. That He is good. All the time. That He can be trusted. That we do not see what He sees. That He loves us and loves Gavin more than we can comprehend. That death has no victory or sting and Gavin truly lives now in Heaven. That God uses every bit of our pain for a purpose.. That God can bring triumph out of any tragedy. That He is always with us, whether we are in a storm, on a mountaintop, or in the valley.

Chapter Five: Peaks and Valleys

* * *

If I had a choice, I would avoid being in an open boat in a raging storm. I would stay out of the valleys of the shadow of death. I much prefer calm seas, where the sun sparkles like diamonds on the small ripples. I also get a rush standing on mountaintops, where the view is incredible. The air is clean, and you feel invincible. I think most people do. But I see the truth in the teaching that contrasts mountaintops and valleys with growth. Think about it. As you climb a mountain, the vegetation gets thinner. The higher you go, the less oxygen there is. The less life can be sustained. On the tallest peaks, there is no growth. No green. None. Nada. Zip. Just cold, hard rock.

Now think about valleys. Cradled in between the peaks, they receive the runoff when icy peaks melt. They get watered and fertilized. They are usually lush and green. Plenty of vegetation grows in the valleys. Lots of life can be sustained there.

The beautiful paradox of faith in God is that He allows life to flourish even when you are surrounded by death. Psalm 34:18 (NIV) says, "The Lord is close to the brokenhearted and saves those who are crushed in spirit." Jeannie and I have found that to be true. On the mountaintop, it's easy to forget that God is there. The wind is blowing your hair back, you feel great, and your sense of achievement is strong. You accomplished something by reaching the top of that mountain. God rarely gets the credit for taking you there.

In the valley, however, you cling to the Lord for dear life. In between your sobs, He is all that sustains you. You cannot go on without Him. His presence feels closer than ever before. You learn more about yourself and more about Him than any mountain top experience could ever teach you.

Gavin made it through Christmas, 2014, but hovered in the valley of the shadow of death from January until his death on April 1, 2015. Still, growth occurred. Life fought to shine through. In January, Gavin and I were sitting on the couch together, and I had the opportunity to share with my son the importance of asking Christ into his life. Gavin had grown up knowing about God, but now I believe he knew he needed God. Although we had not shared with him all the details of his diagnosis, he was now bedridden or spent his days in a wheelchair. He could no longer function like the boy he had been before. He knew something was really wrong, and I had the opportunity to lead him into prayer. He knew he needed to accept Jesus and wanted to go to Heaven. I know he believed the prayer his little boy heart prayed.

In the valley of the shadow of death, the devil did not have the final victory. He did not get the most important part of my boy. Gavin is spending eternity with Jesus. How privileged I feel to have stood with Gavin in that valley as life and death went head-to-head. The Lord (and Gavin) definitely had the victory that day! Cancer may have wasted Gavin's body, but his spirit became healthier than it had ever been before. To God be the glory.

One other note on valleys: if you find yourself in a valley that seems as if it will never end, it is vitally important that you do not quit. Do not quit on God, your family, your occupation, your church, or yourself. In the moment of your greatest struggle, I highly encourage you to turn to God, not from Him. Many people do the opposite. Why? Because the devil has gotten really good at planting a lie in human hearts so that deep down we believe God is not really a good father. Maybe we believe it because we did not have a good human father. Maybe we believe it because we have never opened our hearts and ears to hear God's Spirit before. Whatever the case, when we are knee-deep in the valleys, we tend to act as if God has schemed against us and wants to do evil to us.

However, I am a witness to the fact that God is a good father. The best father. He never plots ways to curse His children. Rather, He constantly finds ways to bless His children. God is right there beside you in the valley, right this very second, trying to show you the way out. Holding your hand and your heart. They are precious to Him. He never leaves you, even when you feel as though you can't find Him. It's easy to act as if God is far from us, when Hebrews 13:5 says, "Let your conduct be without covetousness;

be content with such things as you have. For He Himself has said, 'I will never leave you nor forsake you.'" (NKJV)

Notice the word "never." God *never* leaves or abandons us, in the peaks or in the valleys of life. There is life that springs forth out of the valley when you recognize in your heart and get revelation in your Spirit that He never leaves. He isn't far from you. In fact, He is close to you right now.

Close your eyes. Be very still. Let your heart open to Him. Ask Him to be a tangible presence. Tell Him you need to sense Him. Can you feel Him? Can you feel the warmth of His arms? Can you sense even an inkling of His comfort? I know many of us, myself included, have had people leave us, disappoint us, and hurt us. But our view of natural, person-to-person relationships on this earth should not be the barometer for our supernatural relationship with Jesus Christ. He *never* leaves us!

That means when Gavin was doing well, God never left us. The moment Gavin received the devastating diagnosis, God never left us. That moment I stood over the couch holding Gavin's hand in death, God never left us. This is the truth that can keep you stable in unstable seasons in life. When you grab with all your might even a grain of faith in the valley, you will find peace. You will experience comfort. You will make it through.

But only if you don't quit. So you can't quit now. You've been through too much. Maybe the devil has stolen good thoughts from you and replaced them with a false view of God. And maybe that false view of God and your situation has led you down a long trail of insecurities, doubt, unbelief and so much more.

I am telling you that you can tell those terrible thoughts to get lost. Call out to God and He will answer. There is faith in you that might have been lying there dormant. Wake up! God has placed that measure of faith in you. He is the author and finisher. Let Him come in and write your story. Renew your mind. Transform your life.

Today is your day not to quit. Today is your day to rise up. Don't give up! God desires and wills good for you whether you are on the peak or in the valley. Right now, I want you to say this out loud wherever you are: "God, I thank you that you never leave me and never give up on me. I am and always will be a child of God. I decree and declare I am victorious right now."

If you just said that and all you feel is a little silly for talking out loud to yourself, don't worry. He heard you. So did the devil. Keep resisting. The enemy has to flee. Everytime you speak the Word of God, faith grows and overtakes the attack of the enemy in your mind.

Have you ever been on a plane and experienced turbulence? The plane bucks like a wild stallion. Fear causes you to break out in a cold sweat, and you begin praying whether you usually pray or not. "Oh God, oh God, oh God…" Am I right? If you could open the door and step right off that wild ride, you would. Then you realize that wouldn't work, so you pull your seat belt a little tighter, grit your teeth, and hang on for the ride. Eventually, you get to your destination. We will all experience turbulence in life. But we should never jump out of the plane. Do not quit!

Believe me, I wanted to quit when my little boy left this life. At the same time, however, my wife Jeannie and I also experienced the truth that God is close to the brokenhearted. He was and is right there. He wrapped His arms around us. He gave us enough strength to hang on just a little bit longer. Just another day. Just one more step.

I want to encourage your heart today that God is not distant from you. He is close. He is close to you in your moments of weakness. In your time of sorrow. In the moments when you don't feel Him. So don't run from Him. The next time you stand in the valley, experience turbulence, or struggle in the storm, draw close to God. He is your Abba. Your Dad. Let Him tuck you under His strong arm and pull you close to His heart. When He does, you will feel His heartbeat sustaining you when it feels like yours can't beat another beat.

Still in the Storm: Peaks and Valleys

1. Are you currently on a peak or in a valley? What is God teaching you there?

   _____

   _____

   _____

   _____

   _____

   _____

2. When have you most closely felt God's presence? What was happening in your life?

   _____

   _____

   _____

   _____

   _____

   _____

3. What action steps will you take to keep a measure of faith the next time you want to give up in life?

   _____

   _____

   _____

   _____

   _____

   _____

Still in the Storm: A Prayer for Perseverance

Dear Father in Jesus Name,

I want to thank you first and foremost for being the Lord of my life. I know there are times when life has its ups and downs, peaks and valleys, but today I declare that you are Lord. Lord of the peaks and Lord of the valleys. I thank you that you never change, and that your thoughts towards me are always good. Thank you for being close to me, and never distant.

There may be times where I feel like giving up, but today I am thankful that I do not walk and live my life based on my feelings. I declare I live by faith. I may feel weak, but I thank you that in my weakness your strength is made perfect, and I am getting stronger every day.

God, I am so thankful, that in my life whether I am on top of the mountain or in the lowest valley that you are for me. You show me your faithfulness everyday. Thank you for causing my life to prosper and be in good health as I pursue you on the peaks or in the valleys.

In Jesus's name I pray,
Amen

Peaks and Valleys: The Next Steps

- If you live in a mountainous region, drive or hike to the top of a peak. Look down at the valley below. What do you see? If you do not live where there are mountains, use the Internet to research some mountainous regions. Look at the images. Compare and contrast the peaks and valleys. What differences do you see?

- If you are in an emotional valley of anger, despair, or grief, give yourself a random act of kindness each day this week..

Go to the beach. Take a walk outside. Get a massage. Eat healthy foods. Drink a lot of water. See a friend. Even if you do not feel like doing anything, take steps to preserve your health and to rest.

- Talk to God out loud. He is not going anywhere. When you see signs of His presence, feel His comfort, or receive answers from Him, write these down in a journal or notebook that you can keep as a witness to His faithfulness.

CHAPTER SIX: FAITH, HOPE, AND LOVE

"So these three things continue forever:
faith, hope, and love.

And the greatest of these is love."
1 Corinthians 13:13 (NCV)

You've probably heard 1 Corinthians 13:13 before: "So these three things continue forever: faith, hope, and love. And the greatest of these is love." (NCV) But what does this Scripture really mean? Why does God tie these three ideals, these elements of the spirit, together? How do they work together, and can they exist apart?

When the disciples were scared in the storm, Jesus said they had little faith. We can see from their fear that they lost hope. In one verse, we see all three of these ideals (or the lack of them, in this case) again tied together: faith, hope, and love.

As a minister, I have discovered that telling people to hang on to hope is not nearly enough. In our loss of Gavin, if my wife and I had only held on to hope, we would have become bitter and disillusioned when he died. Our hope would have died too. We would have been just like the disciples in the storm, full of fear. Where there is hope (or an expression of hope) without faith, hope is little more than a fantasy.

Faith is the fuel in the vehicle of hope. The Bible tells us this explicitly. "Now faith is the substance of things hoped for, the evidence of things not seen," Hebrews 11:1 (KJV) says. Faith is what you can hold onto when you hope for things. Faith tells you everything is going to be okay even when your circumstances try to show you that it is not.

My faith in God is the evidence of Gavin's eternal healing, even though I cannot see it right now. My faith is the substance of the hope I have that I will be reunited with my son in Heaven someday. Faith is like the sugar in a hope cookie recipe. It is the substance that makes that hope cookie taste good. You can remove the faith sugar and still have a cookie (sort of), but it won't taste very good. Anyone who bites into one of those cookies would say something vital was missing. Faith sweetens hope with love's promise.

Faith sweetens hope with love's promise.

Faith is the substance of the hope, and love is God's language that expresses and gives us that hope. For believers, faith is the substance that allows us to trust that even in tragedy God causes us to be triumphant.

I have faith to know that Jesus in me is more than enough, even when I may not see any change in my situation. We must "see" the provision of God first in our hearts, so that we can then see it with our eyes. Whatever you need, see it before you see it, in order to see it.

What I mean is this: God wants our hearts before our intellect.

When we trust with our hearts and allow these three ideals to work together in our lives, they move us from a place of despair to a place of promise. They propel us forward from darkness into the light. Hope fueled by faith gives us the ability to pursue our God-given purpose in life and not allow a moment or even a season of crisis to define who we are.

Chapter Six: Faith, Hope, and Love

As I was facing one of my lowest and weakest moments I knew I needed to get away to see a great friend of mine, who lives in Dallas. During this weekend away I attended a church service at Calvary Church, where I was introduced to Pastor Ben Dailey, the Lead Pastor. Calvary is a multi-site Church in the Dallas metroplex area, where thousands gather together every weekend. It was such a life changing service, and it became a defining moment for me personally. As I heard the Word that night all of the weight of heaviness fell off of me, and I walked out of the service with a renewed hope and joy. The Word of God will change you from the inside out. That night, Pastor Ben preached from 2 Corinthians 4:16-18 and I want to share a little bit of this teaching with you.

2 Corinthians 4:16-18, where Paul says:

> "Therefore we do not lose heart. Even though our outward man is perishing, yet the inward man is being renewed day by day. For our light affliction, which is but for a moment, is working for us a far more exceeding and eternal weight of glory, while we do not look at the things which are seen, but at the things which are not seen. For the things which are seen are temporary, but the things which are not seen are eternal."

The Apostle Paul, who wrote the New Testament letters to the Corinthians, is referencing two powerful truths in this passage of scripture. He is speaking of the two realms that we operate in, the seen and the unseen. As humans we think in concepts, so I want to create an image for you. If you will, imagine a line. Above the line is the realm that Paul talks about as the "unseen." It is a realm of faith and belief, a realm that is eternal and not seen. It is a realm where the Spirit is. If I can say it this way, it is the realm above the line.

The second realm Paul talks about is the realm of the "seen." It is a realm of the temporary. Better yet, we can call it the realm of the natural. It is a realm of the senses where you can see, touch, and feel. It is the realm where good and evil operate. The realm where there is movement and action. It is a realm of process and need. It is a realm of the temporary. It has a beginning and an end. It is a realm of past, present, and future. Let me say it this way: it is the realm below the line.

These realms coexist together. If you are picturing that line, above the line is the realm of the eternal and unseen; and below the line is the realm of the seen and temporary. For now, we live below the line. The mistake that many of us make is to think that what is below the line (temporary) is eternal. It's where we live. It's what we can see. So we tend to think it is all there is.

But the temporary is not where we will be forever. We are here for a brief period of time, and what we do for Christ while we are below the line is what will last and transcend into the realm above the line.

Both realms are important. They both matter and they both have a place in our lives. Why? Because God made them both. Make no mistake about it. Paul encourages us in verse 18 not to look at the things that are temporary or seen, but rather to focus on the realm of the unseen or eternal. I'll put it this way: focus on the realm above the line even while still living below the line.

In the middle of my grieving, I began to comprehend this and fully began this journey Paul is talking about. I started to realize that although I live in the realm of the temporary, I must focus on the eternal. When I do this, I am able to dwell both below and above the line, in the realm of the temporary and the eternal. How? By faith.

When adversity comes or challenges arise, the temptation will be to live below the line and stay in doubt. Instead, we must realize that even while living in the temporary realm, there is a realm above the line where faith is.

If you remove this kind of faith from your spiritual life, you will take on the form of a believer in Christ but never have a root that goes deep and anchors you into the rich soil of the love of Jesus Christ. Soon, your belief, your hope, will wither and die.

Like I said in the previous chapter, we have seen many people lose faith in God when something like the death of a child, the loss of a marriage, or financial ruin comes into their lives. When crisis comes, hope quickly runs out of steam. Then the assurance of Christ's love is nowhere to be found. That is just where the devil wants us. It is the devil's intention to get us to walk away from God, rather than run to Him when something like a crisis happens.

Yet it is faith in God when everything goes wrong that pulls your vehicle of hope out of the quicksand of despair. Think of faith as the gasoline that allows your vehicle of hope to go from one point to another. Without it, you cannot go anywhere. You get stuck and eventually that place of being stuck becomes normal rather than abnormal. When a crisis comes and you do not respond with faith, you get stuck in the mire of depression and hopelessness. The devil wants to keep you in that stuck place so that faith won't rise up and give you the hope that Jesus will be your rescue. Instead, fight back and bring on a gas can of faith. Fill up your tank, and the vehicle of hope will propel you once again toward your purpose in life.

* * *

How do we get that kind of faith when our hope is sputtering to a halt? We demonstrate our faith by love. The kind of love God expresses throughout 1 Corinthians 13:1-8 (MSG).

"If I speak with human eloquence and angelic ecstasy but don't love, I'm nothing but the creaking of a rusty gate.

If I speak God's Word with power, revealing all his mysteries and making everything plain as day, and if I have faith that says to a mountain, 'Jump,' and it jumps, but I don't love, I'm nothing.

If I give everything I own to the poor and even go to the stake to be burned as a martyr, but I don't love, I've gotten nowhere. So, no matter what I say, what I believe, and what I do, I'm bankrupt without love.

Love never gives up.

Love cares more for others than for self.
Love doesn't want what it doesn't have.
Love doesn't strut,
Doesn't have a swelled head,
Doesn't force itself on others,
Isn't always 'me first,'
Doesn't fly off the handle,
Doesn't keep score of the sins of others,
Doesn't revel when others grovel,
Takes pleasure in the flowering of truth,
Puts up with anything,
Trusts God always,
Always looks for the best,
Never looks back,
But keeps going to the end.
Love never dies."

I love the end of that. We put up with anything. Trust God always. Look for the best. Never look back and dwell on the problems of the past. And keep going to the end. That means we trust God when we don't feel like it. We love on others when we ourselves feel dried up. We don't fly off the handle. We never, ever give up.

When we are filled with that kind of love, the kind of love we act upon even when we do not feel it, then our faith can move us forward to fulfill our purpose in Christ. Hope is our vehicle, but faith is the substance that fuels it so that God's love can be expressed through our own life story to win others to Christ.

Hope is our vehicle, but faith is the substance that fuels it so that God's love can be expressed through our own life story to win others to Christ.

If we do not learn to have faith, if I do not preach and teach and stand on my faith, then there will not be enough substance in my life to get my vehicle of hope to its proper destination.

Plus, it is my love for God and God's love for me that births in me a love for others. A love for His people. Without love, 1 Corinthians 13 says my words just sound like a rusty, creaking gate. In moments of crisis, we want people to have hope. However, we cannot impart hope to anyone without love.

With the story of Gavin, we consistently remain hopeful and hope-filled. We never become hopeless because we understand the love of God. Gavin's story is not over yet. Through Christ's love, the ability to remain in faith caused us to see the best in our son even when he was at his worst. Because even as his body deteriorated and the evidence of his physical healing was not seen, our faith showed us that Gavin's love and his heart never changed. That nasty, evil tumor never robbed our son of his love for us. It could not take away his faith in God. Therefore, it could never rob us of our hope that Gavin lives on in eternity.

You may feel like you cannot go forward in life, but you can. You can make it, if you grasp even an inkling of His love for you and operate in His love toward others. Again, faith operates by love. Then faith and hope work together through that love.

When the Apostle Paul wrote the letter to the Corinthians church, he wrote all those things in Chapter 13 about love because he was trying to get the Corinthian believers to quit fighting with each other. He was admonishing them for not believing the best in each other. Love believes the best, even when the worst happens. Even when things are going wrong. And faith works by love, so even though tragedy happens, we can still choose through our relationship with God to love others and keep our faith. Which fuels our hope. When faith, hope, and love work in tandem, they keep us moving forward no matter what we see in the circumstances all around us.

* * *

In order to truly understand the part love plays in the faith, hope, and love equation, it is crucial to understand the work Christ did on the cross. The love He displayed. The dispensation of grace that the finished work of the crucifixion gives us. And the position we have because of that finished work. Ephesians 2:8 reveals to us, "For it is by grace you have been saved, through faith--and this is not from yourselves, it is the gift of God" (NIV). In this case, grace is an actual person ... the person of Jesus Christ. By *Jesus* we have been saved through faith. When we can grasp this, we can better understand our position with God. When His only Son died on the cross for my sin, for Gavin's sin, and for your sin, He made us fully and completely reconciled with God once we accept Him through our faith. Despite all the things we have done wrong that damaged our relationship with God, we become whole again with our Creator through his son's obedience and sacrifice. We become full sons and daughters of the King of Kings. As beloved sons and daughters, we are the heirs to His kingdom on earth and in Heaven. We live in an age of grace that will continue for eternity.

In practical terms, we are enough for God. Just like we are. He accepts us because of what Jesus did. He loves us, and He longs for fellowship with us. Through the understanding of our position in Christ, we are finally able to have rest and peace, even in un-restful seasons and chaotic times. The Lord is our *El Shaddai*. In Genesis 17:1, the Lord appears to Abram and changes his name to Abraham. It is here that God refers to Himself for the first time as *El Shaddai,* which is generally accepted to mean He is the Almighty God, the All-Sufficient One, and the one true God. He is letting Abraham know that even though it looks like he and Sarah are too old to have children, God is powerful enough to make Abraham's descendants too numerous to count. With God, everything is possible.

As his treasured sons and daughters, we are to rest in His love when life gives us situations impossible to fix by ourselves. We lean on His might when we are too weak to stand. We trust that He is strong when we are falling apart. We fully rely on the fact that God can supply more than enough to meet any and all of our needs.

In John 10:10, Jesus declares: "The thief comes only in order to steal and kill and destroy. I came that they may have *and* enjoy life, and have it in abundance [to the full, till it overflows]" (AMP). Even though the enemy through cancer came to steal, Jesus came to give life. In Gavin's case, his life continues in eternity. Therefore, even in Gavin's death, we are able to have peace and joy. Through Christ's work on the cross, we can process this tragic season of our family's life with the faith that fuels the hope that we will be reunited with our precious son. That wrongs will be righted. And that God knows and loves us more than we can comprehend while we remain on the earth.

The Word of God tells us that by Jesus stripes (wounds), we are healed (Isaiah 53:5). Not that we are going to remain sick. Not that we will be healed someday. But that we ARE healed. Right now. Present tense. But Jamey, I can hear you asking, how is that possible when my body is still riddled with disease? How can you say that when my heart is still broken because my prodigal child has not come home? You must be kidding when I cannot even conquer this addiction no matter how hard I try. How can you say I am healed? Jamey, how can you believe in healing when your prayers did not result in healing for Gavin?

I tell you that even though all of our prayers, our fasting, our gathering people together worldwide to intercede on Gavin's behalf could be seen by the world as "failing" because Gavin still died, we fully believe God can and does perform miracles today. We know that we know that we know Gavin was healed fully and is rejoicing in his perfect body in Heaven. Were we disappointed that we didn't get to see a miracle like Jesus did here on earth? Of course. Would we rather have seen our son literally raised from the dead to live a long life here with us? Absolutely. I don't have all the answers as to why Gavin did not receive healing in the earthly realm. But my confidence and trust and faith remain in the Word of God.

My personal belief is that God was, is, and always will be a God of miracles, and that's how I can continue to align my faith with others who have cancer or are in need of a miracle. That's how I can still believe that God can choose to heal them here and now. I do not have to understand why some people receive their healing here on the earth and why for some that healing does not happen until they return home to heaven. My job is just to exercise my faith.

Like I said before, in every situation in life we need to have the faith to "see" our miracles before we see them in the flesh. Or in the circumstances. We need to keep telling ourselves we are healed even before we see any evidence of it. We can thank God for our healing even when nothing appears to have changed. God can restore health, relationships, finances, and all of the brokenness in this fallen world. Our job is to believe that for those who have been reconciled to Him, it is already done.

I know this can be a difficult thing to do. As a Christ follower, when you have prayed and believed for something and it didn't happen, or it hasn't happened yet, how do you still process the goodness of God? In the case of our sweet son Gavin, we know in our hearts God didn't want his death to happen. But it happened. The Bible says the devil is running around this world like a roaring lion, seeking those he can devour (1 Peter 5:8). Since his rebellion from God and banishment from Heaven, Satan has had a certain amount of power on this earth. For now. Until Jesus comes again.

I believe God hates what Satan is doing to this earth, but He is holding out as long as He possibly can for more people to come to accept His son Jesus Christ. One day, God will judge this earth. He will judge Satan and his demons. He will cast them into the lake of fire forever. But God does not want any of the people He created to be separated from Him for eternity. And I believe His heart is breaking. Breaking over the sin. Breaking over the sickness. Breaking over the deteriorated state of the once-beautiful creation He made. God's hands are not tied. He is not powerless. He is patient. He is holding back so that more people might come to know and love Him.

That's why Jeannie and I won't let Satan win. He might have robbed Gavin of time on this earth through cancer, but Christ had the ultimate victory as Gavin is in Heaven today. He might try to tear our faith down and our family apart, but he will never be able to do it if we remain strong in our faith. With God for us, who can be against us (Romans 8:31)? The devil would love for us to wallow in Gavin's death until it destroys us. He would love to see us in the depths of depression. I have no doubt he would cackle gleefully if our marriage ended in divorce like so many do after the death of a child. We refuse to give him any more ground. "As for me and my house, we will serve the Lord" (Joshua 24:15).

As sons and daughters of Christ, we can take authority over the devil and tell him to go. How do we exercise authority out of loss and pain? We walk by faith and not by sight (2 Corinthians 5:7). Even when everything is crazy and at its worst. People sometimes say to me, "That is very inspirational." Hear me clearly: I don't want to inspire you. I want to give you spiritual tools and allow God to transform you!

What I know is that I continue to rebuke the enemy. That means I literally tell the devil that he has to leave us alone in Jesus name. Every time he tries to keep me in bed. Every time he tries to keep me discouraged. Every time he makes me feel inadequate to comfort my wife. Every time he tries to tell me I am not good enough, not working hard enough, not anything enough, I tell him in no uncertain terms to back off! And when I do, he flees. James 4:7 gives Christians this authority: "Submit therefore to God. Resist the devil and he will flee from you" (NASB). I submit my will, my natural inclinations, my feelings to God. Then I can command Satan to go away. When I submit myself to God, I am able to recognize when thoughts or feelings are not from God. My spirit is able to say, "Okay, this is not normal. This is another form of attack to split our family, ministry, or house. With God for me, the devil has no power to be against me."

When I resist through my faith in God, the devil has to go. There I find rest. I find peace. There is pure freedom in Christ through a life of faith. In the storm of Gavin's cancer, hope got me in the boat. But faith kept my boat afloat.

We can see this freedom through faith demonstrated in the healing miracles Jesus performed in his earthly ministry. Every time Jesus engaged in a situation with people, not only did he provide for them but also he demonstrated freedom. In most of the Gospel scriptures, we see Jesus preaching, teaching, and performing miracles. What we need to recognize is that the real miracles were not just the bodily healings, the resurrection from the dead, the casting out of demons. No, the real miracle was the freedom received by those who were touched by Jesus. Their lives were transformed forever. Sin forgiven. Lifestyles changed. Yes, bodies were healed. But the rest of their lives … into eternity ... became free. John 8:36 bears witness to this truth: "So if the Son sets you free, you are truly free." When Jesus sets you free from sin, you are truly free. That, my friends, is a real miracle!

When we look at the cross and resurrection of Jesus, His sacrifice allows us to go deeper into a place of understanding of the freedom found in a relationship with Him. Consider the woman in Mark 5:25-34. In this passage of scripture, we find a woman who had suffered from bleeding for twelve years. She had never met Jesus. She had not talked to Him face-to-face. There was no Internet for her to hear about His miracles or research His works on Wikipedia. However, she had heard of Him somehow. And she believed, sight unseen, that He could heal her. To the point that she fought her way through the crowd just to touch the hem of his robe.

"Jesus went with him, and all the people followed, crowding around him. A woman in the crowd had suffered for twelve years with constant bleeding. She had suffered a great deal from many doctors, and over the years she had spent everything she had to pay them, but she had gotten no better. In fact, she had gotten worse. She had heard about Jesus, so she came up behind him through the crowd and touched his robe. For she thought to herself, 'If I can just touch his robe, I will be healed.' Immediately the bleeding stopped, and she could feel in her body that she had been healed of her terrible condition. Jesus realized at once that healing power had gone out from him, so he turned around in the crowd and asked, 'Who touched my robe?' His disciples said to him, 'Look at this crowd pressing around you. How can you ask, "Who touched me?"' But he kept on looking around to see who had done it. Then the frightened woman, trembling at the realization of what had happened to her, came and fell to her knees in front of him and told him what she had done. And he said to her, 'Daughter, your faith has made you well. Go in peace. Your suffering is over.'"

This woman who had suffered for twelve years received freedom for the rest of her life because she was propelled by her faith to seek out Jesus and get so close to Him that she could touch Him. Her freedom was birthed from a place of faith. She believed. She affirmed her faith with her thoughts, telling herself that Jesus could heal her. Then she took action by touching his robe. And she was completely healed. She found freedom.

You can too. Believe. Trust. Align your words and your thoughts with your faith. Then put action to it. The message of faith in God is transformational and can help people all around you move from suffering to a place of wholeness. You can truly experience freedom when you understand that faith can be released through action. It's not an exact science. There is no precise formula. Just keep allowing faith to grow in your heart, then take steps of action wherever the Lord leads. You will experience freedom like you never have before!

Still in the Storm: Faith, Hope, and Love Connection

1. What two new things did you learn in this chapter about the connection between faith, hope, and love?

   _____

   _____

   _____

   _____

   _____

   _____

2. How can you live below and above the line in terms of exercising your faith?

   _____

   _____

   _____

   _____

   _____

   _____

3. What action have you put to your faith? How are you sharing your faith and freedom in Christ with others?

   _____

   _____

   _____

   _____

   _____

   _____

Still in the Storm: A Prayer for Freedom through Faith

Dear Father In Jesus Name,

Thank you for Jesus finished work on the cross. I praise you for your sacrifice for me. Thank you for the freedom I have when I exercise my faith in you. Help me to understand that as I take my thoughts captive and resist the devil that he flees from me.

Thank you that you have given me such freedom in Christ that I do not have to live in worry, doubt, and unbelief. You have given me power to live by faith and focus on the realm of the eternal.

Thank you that my eternity is assured with you. Thank you for loving me unconditionally and giving me the power to focus and live my life in the freedom I have in you. I love you, Lord, and I honor you with my faith, hope, and love. Nothing is impossible for you.

In Jesus Name I pray,
Amen

Faith, Hope, and Love: The Next Steps

- Find five healing miracles Jesus performed in the gospels. Read the stories. Then write down how each Bible character experienced freedom after their encounter with Jesus. Then make a list of the freedoms you have found since giving your life to Christ.

- Design a cross. You can sculpt it out of clay, make a collage, glue together flowers, draw with markers, string a cross out of beads, or use any artistic medium of your choosing. Hang your cross as a reminder that although you are not perfect (just as your handmade cross may not be perfect), Christ's death on the cross makes you perfect in Him.

CHAPTER SEVEN: THE HOLY SPIRIT

"And I will ask the Father, and he will give you another Advocate, who will never leave you. He is the Holy Spirit, who leads into all truth. The world cannot receive him, because it isn't looking for him and doesn't recognize him. But you know him, because he lives with you now and later will be in you. But when the Father sends the Advocate as my representative—that is, the Holy Spirit—he will teach you everything and will remind you of everything I have told you".

– John 14:16-17, 26 (NLT)

When the disciples walked the earth with Jesus, He was beside them. He was with them. But He was not in them. When Jesus fell asleep on the boat and the disciples felt afraid, it was because they forgot about the power of Jesus being with them. They could not see His power. They did not know how to exercise their faith without His active presence. Instead, they feared for their lives.

Up until Christ's death on the cross and His resurrection from the dead, mankind was separated from the presence of God by sin. As I have explained in a previous chapter, only the High priest of the temple could enter the presence of God. Once a year. Behind the temple veil. The priest made a sacrifice, and the people brought their animal sacrifices, so that God would forgive their sins through the shedding of blood. But the people of God did not actively know His presence in their hearts. We see in some Old Testament passages that great men of God like David were visited by the Holy Spirit. But the Spirit of God did not dwell in them.

After Jesus was resurrected, He appeared to His disciples and followers on a number of occasions and continued to teach them for forty days before He ascended to Heaven to sit at the right hand of God on His eternal throne. In John 14, Jesus is telling His followers what will happen after He leaves them. In this passage, we see that Christ wants them to know He is not abandoning them. In fact, for the first time since sin entered the world, human beings will now have direct access to God like they have never experienced before. Jesus says He will pray for His followers that God the Father will send them a Comforter. And in Acts 2, God does. The Holy Spirit descends on the crowd of Christ followers and appears as tongues of fire over their heads.

> "They saw what seemed to be tongues of fire that separated and came to rest on each of them. All of them were filled with the Holy Spirit and began to speak in other tongues as the Spirit enabled them."
>
> – Acts 2:3-4 (NIV)

This is a huge deal. Why? Because the Holy Spirit now indwells, lives within, those who accept Christ. The Holy Spirit, who is the third being of the Trinity. Our three-in-one God. The Holy Spirit is sent to be our Helper. The Bible tells us the Holy Spirit in us comforts us, teaches us, gives us wisdom, and fills us with power.

That's right. We have the power through the Holy Spirit to tell the devil to leave us alone. To exercise our faith. To put action to our faith. To get out of the muck and mire and live in joy, peace, and freedom. Sounds easy, doesn't it? But I know it's not. The enemy gets us stuck again and again. We need to call on our friend, our Helper, the Holy Spirit, to get us unstuck.

Now some people get a little freaked out at the term "Holy Spirit" or "Holy Ghost." They don't want to be seen as one of those "Holy Rollers". I am here to tell you that knowing the Holy Spirit is not about a bunch of "hocus-pocus." No! Knowing the Holy Spirit is the best way to truly become intimate with God.

The Trinity is three-in-one. That means God the Father is fully God. Jesus the Son is fully God. And the Holy Spirit is fully God. You can't have one without the others. You limit your faith severely if you only learn about God the Father and Jesus the Son. You must get to know the Holy Spirit, or your faith will become mere works with no power of God fueling them for His glory.

How can I help de-mystify the Holy Spirit? How can you embrace this third person of God without skepticism? By diving into God's Word to discover the Holy Spirit's plan and purpose in you.

Because He is God, He was, is, and always will be. He is the Alpha and the Omega. The beginning and the end. In the second verse of the Bible, Genesis 1:2, we already see the Holy Spirit at work during the creation process. "Now the earth was formless and empty, darkness was over the surface of the deep, and the Spirit of God was hovering over the waters." (NIV)

The Holy Spirit again is credited with creation power in Psalm 104:30, which states: "Then you send your Spirit, and new life is born to replenish all the living of the earth." (TLB)

The Bible alludes to the relationship between Jesus and the Holy Spirit in Isaiah 11:2 (ESV), in a passage that prophesies about the coming Messiah. "And the Spirit of the Lord shall rest upon him, the Spirit of wisdom and understanding, the Spirit of counsel and might, the Spirit of knowledge and the fear of the Lord." When John the Baptist baptized Jesus in water, we see the full Trinity together when the white dove (a symbol of the Holy Spirit) descends and alights on Jesus, and God the Father's voice expresses his approval of His son. "After his baptism, as soon as Jesus came up out of the water, the heavens were opened to him and he saw the Spirit of God coming down in the form of a dove. And a voice from heaven said, 'This is my beloved Son, and I am wonderfully pleased with him.'" (Matthew 3:16-17, TLB)

The Holy Spirit performs many roles throughout scripture. All are important for us to fully grasp the goodness of the gift of the Holy Spirit to us. The magnitude of such a gift. To be given the Holy Spirit to live within us is better than winning the lottery. Let's look at just a few of the attributes of the Holy Spirit we receive when He comes to live within us:

- Comfort – "But the Helper (Comforter, Advocate, Intercessor—Counselor, Strengthener, Standby), the Holy Spirit, whom the Father will send in My name [in My place, to represent Me and act on My behalf], He will teach you all things. And He will help you remember everything that I have told you." (John 14:26, AMP)

- Strength and Direct Intercession (Prayers to God on our behalf) – "Likewise the Spirit helps us in our weakness. For we do not know what to pray for as we ought, but the Spirit himself intercedes for us with groanings too deep for words." (Romans 8:26, ESV)

- Wisdom, Counsel, Teaching, Understanding, Might, Fear of the Lord, Knowledge – "And the Spirit of the Lord shall rest upon him, the Spirit of wisdom and understanding, the Spirit of counsel and might, the Spirit of knowledge and the fear of the Lord." (Isaiah 11:2, ESV)

- Help – "I will ask the Father, and he will give you another Helper[a] to be with you forever— the Spirit of truth. The world cannot accept him, because it does not see him or know him. But you know him, because he lives with you and he will be in you." (John 14:16-17, NCV)

- Truth – "When the Spirit of truth comes, he will guide you into all truth. He will not speak on his own but will tell you what he has heard. He will tell you about the future." (John 16:13, NLT)

- Freedom – "Now the Lord is the Spirit, and where the Spirit of the Lord is, there is freedom." (2 Corinthians 3:17, NIV)

- Power – "And you know that God anointed Jesus of Nazareth with the Holy Spirit and with power." (Acts 10:38, NLT)

- Boldness to Speak of the Word of God – "And when they had prayed, the place in which they were gathered together was shaken, and they were all filled with the Holy Spirit and continued to speak the word of God with boldness." (Acts 4:31, ESV)

- Life – "The old written covenant ends in death; but under the new covenant, the Spirit gives life." (2 Corinthians 3:6, NLT)

- God's Love – "For we know how dearly God loves us, because he has given us the Holy Spirit to fill our hearts with his love." (Romans 5:5, NLT)

And these verses barely scratch the surface of what Scriptures say regarding the Holy Spirit's role in our lives! Perhaps most importantly, the evidence of the Holy Spirit in us plays out in the "fruit" we display, according to Galatians 5:22-23: "But the fruit of the Spirit is love, joy, peace, longsuffering, kindness, goodness, faithfulness, gentleness, self-control.

Against such there is no law." (NKJV) Who doesn't want their lives to be filled with every one of these qualities and more?

Allowing the Holy Spirit to take up residence in you does not automatically mean you will begin immediately speaking in languages you do not understand, seeing a tongue of fire over your head, or casting demons out of people. While there is much discussion in different denominations over the ways the Holy Spirit reveals Himself in us today, there is one thing every believer in Christ should be able to agree on: that falling in love with the Holy Spirit will open your spiritual eyes and ears to much more of the realm of the eternal.

My best advice is that you be open to anything and everything God has for you – soak up every single thing He has to offer. Be willing to experience the power of the Holy Spirit and see what He can do. To be honest, I pray "in the Spirit" all the time. What does that mean for me? That I allow the Holy Spirit to pray through me in a prayer language I do not understand like I do my native English. However, when I allow these sounds and syllables to leave my mouth in praise and prayer to God, a supernatural peace washes over me. I feel closer to God than I ever have before when I am praying in my prayer language. I don't say this to scare you off, but to encourage you not to put limits on a limitless, all-powerful God!

There are no limits to an almighty, omniscient, omnipresent, triune God. But we limit our own spiritual understanding if we refuse to allow ourselves to know and experience His Spirit and if we refuse to give God's Spirit permission to work in and through us in whatever way He chooses.

He's dwelling in us, but we need to acknowledge Him. We need to make our body, His temple, an inviting place to be. "Do you not know that your bodies are temples of the Holy Spirit, who is in you, whom you have received from God? You are not your own." (1 Corinthians 6:19, NIV)

What I can promise you from my own experience is that if you issue the Holy Spirit an open invitation to have His will and His way in your life, you will receive more than you could ever ask or imagine. You will be stronger in your weakest moments. You will have peace in the midst of chaos. You will find joy when you used to be frustrated. You will love where you used to feel disgust. You will find comfort when you grieve. You will understand more of God than you ever have before. You will want more of God than you ever have before. You will speak about God with a new boldness and confidence. And you will know without a doubt that you are loved, you are wanted, and you are never alone.

Still in the Storm: The Holy Spirit

1. When did you first invite the Holy Spirit into your life? If you have never asked Him to have His way in your life, are you ready to now? Why or why not?

   _____

   _____

   _____

   _____

   _____

   _____

2. What did you learn in this chapter that you did not know about the Holy Spirit before?

   _____

   _____

   _____

   _____

   _____

3. In what ways can you go deeper in your relationship with the Holy Spirit? What attributes of His would you like to see strengthened in your life?

   _____

   _____

   _____

   _____

   _____

Still in the Storm: An Invitation to the Holy Spirit

Dear Father In Jesus Name,

I thank you for giving me the Holy Spirit. I thank you that the Holy Spirit dwells in me, and causes me to be at peaceful in situations that are not peaceful. I thank you that I have joy even when the circumstances say I should be sad, and that I am strong when I should feel weak. Thank you Holy Spirit for empowering me to succeed in every area of life, and for always being my guide. I personally invite you to have full access to my heart so that my life will be a witness and example of Christ to all I come in contact with. I thank you that as I go about each day and as I walk through life that you are with me at all times. I am so hungry and thirsty for the Holy Spirit to saturate my heart. Thank you for living within me, and interceding on my behalf. Teach me to surrender to you, for your ways are higher than mine. I invite you to take me deeper, and help me soar higher. Give me everything you have for me in this life, and help me prepare others for the next life. Give me boldness to declare your name to others, to share my story of your comfort and care in my life.

The Bible says that the same power that raised Jesus from the dead lives in me through you. I want to experience your power. Help me be open to you in new ways. Teach me, lead me, guide me. I allow you to have more of your way, not my own. I invite you to baptize me with your fire, your strength, and your power.

In the power and might of Jesus I pray,
Amen.

The Holy Spirit: The Next Steps

- Ask the Lord to give you an open heart and mind. Read Acts 2:1-4 (NLT). What did you see, hear, and feel? What did you learn?

- Talk to other believers about the Holy Spirit. How have they encountered Him in their lives? How does He reveal Himself? Have they ever "spoken in tongues" or a "prayer language"? What was it like? What do they feel it adds to their spiritual walk? I know this may seem uncomfortable because many have misrepresented the authenticity of the Holy Spirit. I ask you to have a open heart and ask the Holy Spirit to fill you. As you do, I believe you will be filled with a fresh power that can only come from Him.

- If you have never asked God to "baptize" you in the Holy Spirit, make the decision to do so. Invite the Holy Spirit to manifest in you in any way He chooses.

- Do your own personal study of the Holy Spirit. Use commentaries, Bible studies, and Scriptures to help you get to know Him more.

PART THREE: FAITH AS OUR LIFESTYLE

CHAPTER EIGHT: PUT YOUR ARMOR ON

"To appoint unto them that mourn in Zion, to give unto them beauty for ashes, the oil of joy for mourning, the garment of praise for the spirit of heaviness; that they might be called trees of righteousness, the planting of the LORD, that he might be glorified."

- Isaiah 61:3 (KJV)

Faith became my foundation when I was a teenager. It became my freedom as I entered my adult years, I was released from the baggage and emotional bondage left from my childhood and adolescence. But I believe it truly became my lifestyle after my faith was put to the ultimate test with the loss of my little boy. Could my faith survive when all hope was lost?

About two weeks after Gavin died, that moment of testing came for me. The funeral services and all the "busyness" that comes after a death in the family were over. Visitors had all gone home. Jeannie and my other two kids were out for the afternoon running errands, and I was alone in my too-quiet house for one of the first times since Gavin had passed. I put some worship music on and tried to pray, and it truly hit me. Gavin was really gone. Gone from this earth. Gone from my life until eternity. Up until that moment, a lot of what had happened to our family felt like a blur. Now here I was, sitting in my favorite brown leather chair in our living room surrounded by all that was familiar, staring across from my chair at the couch. The empty couch. The one where Gavin used to sprawl all the time. My heart shattered. I felt lost. I felt discouraged and deeply despairing. My thoughts whirled. How had we gotten here? My eight-year-old boy was gone. My family and friends had all returned to their normal lives, their normal routines. But our family was stuck with a new normal we never asked for or wanted. What was I supposed to do now? I began to feel agitated and frustrated. This wasn't fair! I got up and turned off the worship music and sat back down in my chair. My Bible lay unopened next to me on the end table under the lamp. I stopped trying to pray. I sat there, unmoving, and waited. For what? I didn't know. I don't think I was consciously challenging God. But I know now I was waiting for Him to show up. To make some sense of this mess. I don't know how long I sat there, but suddenly I heard a voice in my spirit saying, "Be still." I knew it was God's voice, and I knew He was reminding me of the way He often shows up. In silence. In stillness. In the waiting. When we slow down and are quiet, He can talk. And we are ready to hear.

"Be still and know that I am God," God said in Psalm 46:10 (NIV). In the Gospels' story of the storm that I have referenced throughout this book, Jesus woke up and simply told the storm, "Be still." And it did.

So when God showed up and told me, "Be still," I knew deep within me that He was calming my storm. Commanding the waves of despair not to carry me away from Him. I obeyed. I'm not sure how long I sat there in that chair. Maybe an hour, maybe two. But I was still. Quiet. Listening. Waiting. Eventually, I began to pray again. It took every ounce of energy and self-discipline in me. Honestly, I did not want to talk to God. It would have been a lot easier to let my feelings of grief run rampant. To stay frustrated. To stay in my despair. I mustered up everything I had and surrendered to what the Lord wanted from me. I opened my hurting heart and let Him minister to me. At that time, I know the Holy Spirit in me began to pray through and for me. I prayed in my own prayer language, and I believed with all my heart the Holy Spirit was showing up and doing His job as my Comforter, my Counselor.

The only way I know how to put into words what that prayer time was like is to give you the analogy of a big, painful, sore. It needs a bandage, but putting a bandage on it in that condition will just cover up the infection. It will probably get worse instead of better. To heal, the wound needs to be cleaned. The infection has to come out. Antibiotic ointment needs to be applied. Finally, the bandage can offer protection while the wound heals.

That prayer session felt like the Lord putting triple antibiotic ointment on the gaping hole in my heart. Make no mistake about it. The wound was still there. But His Spirit began to soothe it like supernatural ointment. I found a measure of peace even though I still didn't understand. It was in that intense time of seeking and prayer in my brown leather chair in my living room that I began to know my faith would not waver in this crisis. My family would not be destroyed. In fact, faith would become my lifestyle in a way it never had before. That time of prayer birthed in me the desire to reach out to others and help build their faith. Out of the ashes of Gavin's death, the Lord began to bring beauty. In that special time of stillness and prayer, the dream of a ministry called Faith Builders International was born (More on Faith Builders in Chapter 9).

While sitting in silence, purpose and direction came for the future. I wasn't asking God for it. I was just trying to get some quiet time with Him to allow Him to embrace my heartache and pain. Yet as I released my pain to Him in tearful prayer, it allowed Him to release His purpose to my heart.

Yet as I released my pain to Him in tearful prayer, it allowed Him to release His purpose to my heart.

When we are experiencing the most intense emotions of fear, anger, grief, and despair, I believe it is crucial to be still. To force ourselves to ask Him to come in and have His way in us. Only if we wave the white flag of surrender can He begin the healing work that needs to take place in us. It's not fun at first. Cleaning wounds hurt. It's uncomfortable at best. Yet that surrender becomes the beginning of a real lifestyle of faith. Faith that will stand the test of time, grow continually, and bring others into it.

* * *

What do you think happened to the disciples' faith after Jesus woke up and calmed the storm? The Word of God says they made it to the other side of the lake. But then what did they do? How did they act? What did they think about Jesus? Did that one storm make a difference in the disciples' belief in Jesus and what He could do? I think it did.

Before the incident in the boat, the disciples had already witnessed on many occasions the supernatural power Jesus commanded. In the first chapters of the Gospel of Matthew before the story of the storm is laid out in chapter eight, Jesus cast out evil spirits, healed "many people" including Simon's (Peter's) mother-in-law, and cured a man of the dreaded disease leprosy. Jesus had been preaching and teaching. He had already taught crowds what we now call the Beatitudes and what we know as "The Lord's Prayer," with the disciples in tow to see and hear it all. To soak it all in. They had a front row seat to witness all of Jesus's power and wisdom at work everywhere they went. Then the storm came, and they freaked out.

I believe that after Jesus told his closest friends they had little faith, those friends set out to change. Jesus challenged them in the moment of their storm to grow their faith from that day forward. With the exception of Judas Iscariot, who eventually betrayed Jesus, I believe the Bible shows us they did. Maybe they watched Him a little more closely. Listened to His words more intently. Tried a little harder to process all the radical new ways of living He was teaching them. When He stilled the storm, I believe the disciples became still too – watching in awe as Jesus's power worked its wonders right before their very eyes.

How can I tell that the storm in their lives made a difference in their faith? Because eventually almost all of those disciples died as martyrs for their belief in Jesus as the Christ, the Messiah. Their faith grew and grew after Jesus called them out, and they continued to follow Him for the rest of His life, ministry, death, resurrection, and beyond. Their strong faith impacted the world from the time Jesus lived on the earth until today and for the rest of time.

In the middle of my storm of losing Gavin, I had a choice about my faith too. I could give up, say that God is no longer good or does not have the power He claims to have. I could turn my back on everything I believed in and spent my life since my teenage years serving and pursuing. I could curl up in my grief and become bitter, angry, and hard. Or I could choose to watch Him a little more closely. Listen to His words more intently. Try a little harder to process the radical ways His Word tells me to live. In short, I could choose spiritual death to go hand-in-hand with the death of my son. Or I could choose life in Christ, despite the death of my son.

I choose life.

I choose faith.

But that doesn't mean it's always easy.

∗ ∗ ∗

As I was working on this book, I realized it might sound at times as if Gavin's death did not really tear me up. That my steadfast faith was too good to be true, almost unbelievable. Please believe me, I grieve. I cry. I hurt so bad I can barely breathe at times. I have wailed in agony and cried out for peace. But the point I keep trying to make to you is my honest experience with God throughout everything that happened to our family. I am a living, breathing testimony to the fact that He was always there. That the Lord is close to the brokenhearted. After Gavin's death, I kept my eyes fixed on Him and tried with every fiber of my being not to waver. By keeping faith, God drew close to Jeannie and me. He will draw close to you too.

In the previous chapters in this book, I have taken you on a journey of faith. Faith as the very foundation upon which we build our lives. Faith as the freedom we can find in surrendering to Christ and welcoming in the Holy Spirit. But after the death of Gavin, I had to make faith my lifestyle like never before. My faith had to become so much more than a set of beliefs, an ideal to study, or a temporary fix to my problems. Jesus had to become (and remain) what my family centered our lives around. Jesus had to undergird everything, support everything, and permeate everything. How do we hold onto faith when life feels so hard? How do we fully rely on God and what we believe about Him when everything falls apart? How does faith become our lifestyle no matter what comes against us in this life?

My wife Jeannie and I believe faith can only become strong enough to bear it all when you put your trust in Jesus, while putting on your spiritual armor to stand. You have to dress yourself from top to bottom in His truth, His love, and His wisdom. You have to read His Word when you don't feel like it, put on the "garment of praise" and worship His holiness when you do not even feel like He is there, and talk to Him more than ever when you do not know what to say. Only then can He bring beauty from the ashes of your traumas, your tragedies. Only then can He bring you the oil of joy for mourning.

We have found that faith becomes our lifes expression because of love. We simply want to trust and believe because we love God. Faith and Christianity are not a formula. There are no instructions except to BELIEVE! We believe God because we love Him, and we know that He loves us. When we do these things, our burden of grief is easier to bear. Don't get me wrong. The loss of Gavin will always be with us. Tears and heartache are permanently woven into the fabric of our family. The hole Gavin left will never be filled in this life. However, we grieve with glimmers of sunlight shining through the dark emotions. We suffer knowing Christ our Healer and the Holy Spirit our Comforter are alongside us, giving us strength to go on.

Part of the reason I did not question God's faithfulness through our tragedy, I believe, is the years (decades) I spent getting to know Him. Along the way, I discovered that prayer, praise, and reading the Bible are the key components that can activate your faith and keep it strong no matter what your circumstances are. These three work hand-in-hand to lift you out of your circumstances, bolster your faith, and allow you to hang on to God even when you feel like all hope is lost. Through the study of His Word, continuous communication with Him in prayer, and praising God despite what is happening around you, you will experience peace in your darkest valley. And you can remain close to God on the mountaintops too.

* * *

When you hit a roadblock in life so big and painful that you can't get over, under, around or through it by yourself, prayer becomes your lifeline. While the Bible tells us in 1 Thessalonians 5:17 (NKJV) to "pray without ceasing," as humans we often forget to talk to God when the going is good. But put just about anybody in a foxhole with shots ringing out all around, and prayers issue forth. Even unbelievers often cry out to God when all hope is gone. Our spirits are hardwired to communicate with Him when we are in terror and in pain. Talking to God keeps us upright in the valleys.

So now I'm going to put you right on the spot: What's your prayer life like? Do you talk to God daily? Multiple times a day? When you talk to Him, what do you sound like? Do you give Him a laundry list of requests for yourself, your family, and the people you know? Do you offer a few "thank yous" for your food, your family, and the good things you have and go about your day? Do you have a dedicated time and place each day to have a real heart-to-heart with your Creator, then continue a running dialogue with Him the rest of your waking hours? Is God the first one you talk to when you open your eyes and the last one you turn to when you close them to sleep?

I'm telling you right now, prayer needs to be the bedrock of your lifestyle of faith. James 4:8 (NKJV) tells us: "Draw near to God and He will draw near to you." How do we draw near to God? By talking to Him and listening for His voice.

How do we draw near to God? By talking to Him and listening for His voice.

If you are new to prayer, it might feel strange at first. But you'll get used to it. You can talk out loud or to yourself. You can talk to Him in your closet, your shower, or your car. The point is to start talking to God. To ask and expect Him to start talking back to you.

If you have been a lifelong person of prayer but do not feel like your prayers have been particularly effective or powerful, there is no better time than now to step up your prayer game. Ask Him to expand your prayer life like never before. Wherever you are in your prayer life, let me give you some suggestions that have been helpful to me in drawing near to God. First, determine to talk to God before your feet hit the floor each morning. Greet Him as a best friend. Give your day to Him before it even starts, and He will take you places better than you imagined.

Next, dedicate a specific amount of time to prayer daily. It takes self-discipline to create this habit, but it packs an enormous payoff in your lifestyle of faith. Many people prefer to have their prayer time in the morning in order to feel like they have put God first in their day. However, you may not be a morning person, or your schedule may feel too crowded in the morning to give God the full time and attention He so deserves. Maybe afternoons while the kids are at school and the baby is napping work best for you. Perhaps you feel most alive late at night and want to end your day conversing with your best friend. Whatever time you choose, the point is to make prayer a priority in your day.

Remember, it is really tough to build a relationship with someone you never talk to. Your relationship with God is certainly no exception. The more you talk together, the more you learn His voice speaking to your spirit, the closer you will become, the more assured you will be that your life is in His hands, the more comforted you will be when situations seem beyond your control.

Try to create a quiet, beautiful, uncluttered space where you can spend your alone time with God. Some convert their closets into small sitting rooms. Others have a favorite chair, like my brown leather recliner in our living room. Maybe you like to be outdoors and spend your prayer time marveling at the beauty of creation in the woods or at the beach. Mostly, you just want to find a place where you won't be interrupted or distracted. Create or discover a place where your heart feels comfortable and open to the Holy Spirit. It should be a place where you can hold the chaos of life at bay, push your cares aside, and begin the conversation that will feed your spirit.

If you need to build up the self-discipline of prayer, I suggest starting with at least thirty minutes in continuous prayer daily. You don't have to keep up your end of the conversation the whole time. In fact, don't. Thank God for His presence. Ask the Holy Spirit to speak to you and move within you. Then sit quietly and wait. Of course, if you have urgent prayer needs, talk to God about them. But make it a priority to listen for Him too. If you find your thoughts wandering, ask God to help you bring them back to focus on Him again.

I believe the devil hates prayer. He wants to keep us separated and distant. So don't be surprised if you suddenly find yourself going over your to-do list, thinking about your kids, or wanting to get up and do something else in the middle of your prayer time. Refocus and try again. Each time you do, you are flexing your prayer muscles, building them up and increasing their power.

Some people like to keep a notebook or notepad handy as a "prayer journal" in which to jot down prayer requests and any words, phrases, verses, or visions the Lord seems to speak to them during their prayer time. A prayer journal is a great way to see how the Lord works through your life over time. When a prayer is answered, you can see and remember it. Prayer journals can also become a legacy of your lifestyle of faith to minister to your family for generations to come.

Another suggestion I have for you in regards to prayer, a really important one, is for you to be fully open to whatever the Lord wants to do in your prayer life. By that I mean give God permission to manifest or display Himself in and through you in whatever ways He chooses. If God is infinite, omniscient, and all-powerful, then why would we limit Him in what He can do with us?

I personally came to the conclusion a long time ago that I cannot and will not limit what God wants to do with me. I give Him full reign in my life. Full control. He can show up and show off in me however, whenever, He wants to. Please do not close the book here. I ask that you keep reading, because I am a living testimony to the power that prayer has in my life. It has changed my heart, my family, my friends, and my faith. It has grown me and matured me. It has given me peace and passion and purpose when I could have walked away from it all. I know you've heard this saying before, but it is powerful and true: Prayer changes things.

I will never forget one particular prayer time that was a game-changer for me. I was attending Rhema Bible College, and I played on the basketball team. Our coach was Coach Ivey, and he was a mighty man of prayer. For the first thirty minutes of every basketball practice, our team would pray. We would pray "in the Spirit." Every single practice. The Apostle Paul says in God's Word that we pray out the mysteries of God. And the mysteries bring about revelation. All that means is that even if we don't understand what our spirit is praying to God, whether it is in a prayer language or in utter stillness, God reveals Himself and the ways He is working in our lives.

Well, one day our basketball team took a several-hour bus ride from Tulsa, Oklahoma, down to Louisiana for a basketball game. Our bus was a really nice tour bus, with bunk beds and TVs. I was looking forward to kicking back and relaxing, enjoying that ride and the camaraderie with the guys on the team. We all thought we were going to hang out and chill out. Coach Ivey had other plans. About an hour into the trip, he called us together and said, "Boys, we're going to pray in the Spirit for the next couple of hours." We all thought, "You gotta be kidding, right?" Coach Ivey was deadly serious. I still remember what he said next. He said, "You have got to learn the difference between when you are in the natural and when the spirit of God works in the supernatural. That's when you are praying out the perfect will of God."

We began to pray, and two hours turned into almost three hours. When you start to really pray like that, you forget where you are. You forget everything else when you are yielding your heart like that. I don't remember all of my college basketball games. I'm not even sure I remember who won that particular game. But I distinctly remember those hours of prayer, of losing myself in the mystery of the supernatural. I believe that I prayed things that day I am walking in today. When you surrender yourself like that, you begin to walk with the Lord in ways that strengthen your faith for the rest of your days. After Gavin died and I was sitting alone in my living room that day, I began to pray in the same surrendered way I did on that tour bus on the way to that basketball game. And I actually remembered that prayer session on the bus. Sitting in my chair after Gavin died, God began to show me some of those moments of my past where He was with me. And to remind me that He has already been in my future and is with me then too. He is my past, my present, and my future. He is the Alpha and the Omega, the beginning and the end. Deep, intense prayer sessions give God the opportunity to show you some of the intersections in time when your faith has changed your life.

Deep, intense prayer sessions give God the opportunity to show you some of the intersections in time when your faith has changed your life.

I don't know how to explain what it is like to pray with or "in" the Holy Spirit except that for me it goes something like this: I live in Orlando, but I used to live in Kansas City. I am not in Kansas City anymore and have not lived there for a long time, but I can still tell you what buildings are on the four corners of the intersection of 119th Street and Metcalf. How can I do that? Because I have been there. I know that intersection.

Prayer is like that. It takes us from where we are to where we are going. When you have an active prayer life and you are activating your faith as your lifestyle, your future is no surprise. When you step into new things in your life, it's like you have already "been there" in prayer. You have "seen" it before you see it. That day in my chair it was like that. God began to unveil moments of my life and remind me that none of the events that had taken place or would ever take place were a surprise to Him. That revelation began to birth in me a new peace. I could still dislike the fact that

Gavin was gone with everything in me. But I also knew that I knew that God had a plan before, during, and after for my life. For my family's life. For an abundant life in Him. I am not telling you that you have to pray in a language you do not understand. I cannot force you to keep turning the pages of this book or convince you that the gifts of the Holy Spirit are as real and powerful today as they were on the day of Pentecost when tongues of fire rested on top of the believers' heads and they began speaking in other languages. God instituted prayer, so that His Spirit could come upon people and be with them after Jesus went back to Heaven. In fact, Jesus specifically told His followers the Holy Spirit was coming so that we would not be left alone when Jesus was gone. What I can tell you is that for me, this kind of "Spirit-filled" prayer has been a wonderful gift. Let me put it to you like this: as a kid when you saw the stacks of presents bursting out from underneath the Christmas tree on Christmas morning, would you open only a few of the ones with your name on them and say you did not believe the rest of them were for you? Would you leave them wrapped and sitting under the tree? Or would you tear the pretty paper and bows away and enjoy every gift that had been purchased for you?

God gave us the gift of His son's death on the cross for our sins. The gifts of redemption and grace. He gives us the gifts of being His sons and daughters, heirs to His kingdom. He gives us the gifts of His promises of joy, peace, and all the fruits of the Spirit. And I believe one of His most blessed gifts to me has been the ability to allow the Holy Spirit to pray through me in the language He wants to speak, to connect me in relation-ship with the God who loves me in a way I could not connect by myself. I'm so glad I did not leave that gift unopened, and I encourage you to ask the Lord in your prayer time if there are any gifts He still has for that you have inadvertently left under His tree.

Prayer can be creative as well. You can pray in song, write your prayers, or draw pictures. You can walk while you pray or sit very, very still. I encourage you to expand your prayer life in new ways. Pray longer.

Pray in different places. Pray with more people. Pray in ways you have never prayed before. Prayer is critical to your faith lifestyle. The more you pray, the less distractible you will be. The more you pray and the deeper you go in prayer, the more you will want to pray. The more you pray, the more answers to prayer you will recognize. The more you pray, the easier it will be to discern God's voice speaking to you. I'll say it again: Prayer changes things.

* * *

The second component to faith as a lifestyle is the study of God's Word. God's Word is a love letter to us, a blueprint for us, a storybook filled with life lessons for us to learn. Ephesians 6:10-18 teaches us that we need to put on the full armor of God, an arsenal of armor and weapons He gives us, in order to fend off the devil's attacks. Here is what that passage says in the New Century Version: "Finally, be strong in the Lord and in his great power. Put on the full armor of God so that you can fight against the devil's evil tricks. Our fight is not against people on earth but against the rulers and authorities and the powers of this world's darkness, against the spiritual powers of evil. That is why you need to put on God's full armor. Then on the day of evil you will be able to stand strong. On your feet wear the Good News of peace to help you stand strong. And also use the shield of faith with which you can stop all the burning arrows of the Evil One. Accept God's salvation as your helmet, and take the sword of the Spirit, which is the word of God. Pray in the Spirit at all times with all kinds of prayers, asking for everything you need. To do this you must always be ready and never give up. Always pray for all God's people."

This passage packs a powerful punch for me. It tells me in verse thirteen that I need all these pieces of armor on so I can stand strong in the "day of evil," and what could be more evil than cancer taking a precious son's life? It reminds me that there is a real enemy of my soul who wants to ruin my life here on earth. He wants to ruin it so I will be ineffective in telling others about my faith. He wants to ruin my witness so that I cannot share the powerful message of faith that I have in Christ. Every day, I am not really fighting traffic that frustrates, grief that threatens to turn into depression, money worries, or relationship struggles. I am actually fighting the devil and his demons, the "powers of this world's darkness," who orchestrate and take joy in all the chaos they can cause on this earth. The devil knows I love Jesus. He knows I have accepted Him into my heart and made Him ruler of my life. He knows I am going to join Christ as His bride in Heaven someday. So what does he have left to attack? My faith. My attempts to be a disciple and bring others into the faith.

When I pull out my "sword of the Spirit, which is the Word of God," I can put a stop to the devil and his demons. I can stand on the truth of God's promises holding strong to the stories of faith of those who have gone before me. Like Joseph. And Abraham. Like Elijah. And Noah. But only if I read God's Word. Only if I know its contents. Only if I put them into practice in my life. I have heard many pastors say, "A clean Bible equals a dirty Christian, and a dirty Bible equals a clean Christian." That may be a little simplistic, but the sentiment is very accurate. If your Bible is in pristine condition, you probably have not spent time daily poring over its pages. If there are no creases, folds or markings, you may not be putting God's Word to work enough in your life. You have to lift your sword, use your sword, in order for it to fend off any attacks that come against you.

One interesting fact to me is that the Bible is described as the sword of the Spirit, which attests once again to the importance of this third person in the Trinity. The Holy Spirit wields wisdom, comfort, and counsel. These are powerful weapons to use to protect your mind, your heart, and your body from the devil's attacks. While we experience great challenges in the seen and temporary realm, we can base our thoughts and actions on what God has already spoken through his Word.

Need comfort? Turn to the Psalms. Need to know how to conduct your life, personally and professionally? Pore over the Proverbs. Want to read about the way romantic love should look in marriage and in our marriage to Jesus Christ? Read the Song of Songs (also called the Song of Solomon). Want to learn about Jesus Himself and know His story and teachings? Study the four Gospels. Nothing can replace the daily reading of God's Word in your life, working hand-in-hand with prayer, to grow and mature your faith as your lifestyle.

There are literally thousands, if not millions, of tools available to help you study the Word of God. You can read the same passage in different translations, as I have quoted from different translations in this book. Websites like BibleGateway.com and BibleStudyTools.com can give you verses in different translations side-by-side or even by topic. You can get Bibles organized chronologically or laid out so you can read them all the way through in one year. There are archaeological Bible with extra maps and historical findings; devotional Bibles with prayers and daily readings; contemporary language translations like The Living Bible; and study Bibles with plenty of extra helps for you to learn more about each book's author, context, and history.

You can dig deeper into specific biblical characters or books with tools from popular bible teachers. Listen to audio Bibles and teachings as you drive or when you go to sleep. There are endless ways to study God's Word, your sword of the Spirit, so that it can work in your life to defend you from attacks. I urge you to make prayer and Bible reading utmost priorities in your life, so you can stand strong and still in any of life's storms.

* * *

The third element that keeps faith operating in my life is praise and worship. I am talking about more than music, although music is a powerful tool to cut through the noise of life and usher us into God's presence. I mean full-on giving glory to the King of Kings and Lord of Lords with my words and thoughts. In Isaiah 61:3, the verse I chose for the beginning of this chapter, it tells us God gives us "the garment of praise for the spirit of heaviness," that the Lord may be glorified. The Bible tells us repeatedly to praise God. It says He created us for His glory, to display His creativity, majesty, and power. We would not exist without Him. He longs for our recognition, our praise of Him. Why? Is God just some egomaniacal spirit who needs His self-esteem built up all the time by human beings? Of course not!

God desires for us to praise Him because He knows praise lifts us out of the gloom-and-doom of our circumstances. Worship gets us out of ourselves and into the supernatural. It reminds us there is more than this life. It connects us in relationship to God. We praise Him for all the good things He has given us, for all the works He has done in and through us, and for all the great things to come. God created us to worship Him and give Him glory. We do not worship Him for the benefits we receive, but for who He is. However, because of the infinite grace, love, and mercy God displays towards us, we receive benefits of hope, healing, faith, and freedom when we worship.

The other day in church I was thinking in my heart while we were worshipping about just how much freedom there is when we worship in faith. Worship will deliver us from dark places. In Acts 16:16-40 the Bible tells a story about Paul and Silas that demonstrates the power of praise and prayer. The two Christ-followers encountered a demon-possessed slave girl. They commanded the demons to come out of her, and the demons did. The slave girl's masters dragged Paul and Silas before the local judges and accused them of doing things against Roman laws because they had commanded the demons come out of the girl in the name of Jesus. When they were taken before the judges, here's what happened next: "A mob was quickly formed against Paul and Silas, and the judges ordered them stripped and beaten with wooden whips. Again and again the rods slashed down across their bare backs; and afterwards they were thrown into the prison. The jailer was threatened with death if they escaped, so he took no chances, but put them into the inner dungeon and clamped their feet into the stocks. Around midnight, as Paul and Silas were praying and singing songs to the Lord—and the other prisoners were listening—suddenly there was a great earthquake; the prison was shaken to its foundations, all the doors flew open—and the chains of every prisoner fell off!" (Acts 16:22-25-, TLB, emphasis added)

See what happened there? Prayer and worship were so powerful they caused an earthquake that gave Paul and Silas their freedom. The power of their prayers and praise was so great the earthquake even released everyone else in the jail! There is freedom in praise, power when we worship in the name of Jesus. When we live in a state of worship and prayer to the point that it brings us this freedom and power, others are saved because they want what we have. In the rest of that story in Acts, the jailer decides to kill himself rather than be killed because he knows all the prisoners are going to escape and he will be blamed. Instead, Paul stops him from harming himself and lets the jailer know that all the prisoners are still there. The jailer was so moved he fell down and "begged" Paul and Silas to tell him how to be saved.

"They replied, 'Believe on the Lord Jesus and you will be saved, and your entire household.' Then they told him and all his household the Good News from the Lord. That same hour he washed their stripes, and he and all his family were baptized. Then he brought them up into his house and set a meal before them. How he and his household rejoiced because all were now believers! The next morning the judges sent police officers over to tell the jailer, 'Let those men go!' So the jailer told Paul they were free to leave." (Acts 16:31-36, TLB)

Worship breaks every chain of discouragement, sets captives free, heals every hurt. This was and is a key component for Jeannie and me and our family as we walk through our new normal without Gavin. God made us to fellowship with Him. He loved to walk with Adam and Eve in the Garden of Eden until sin separated man from God. Jesus came to rebuild that intimate relationship, and we come into God's presence today through praise and worship. Moses and the Israelites praised God with song after they miraculously crossed the Red Sea and escaped the cruel oppression and slavery of the Egyptians. Exodus 15:2 (NCV) says, "The Lord gives me strength and makes me sing; he has saved me. He is my God, and I will praise him. He is the God of my ancestors, and I will honor him." After Moses received the Ten Commandments from God, he reminds the people of Israel in Deuteronomy 10 of the praise and honor they should give God as His due: "And now, Israel, what does the Lord your God require of you except to listen carefully to all he says to you, and to obey for your own good the commandments I am giving you today, and to love him, and to worship him with all your hearts and souls? Earth and highest heaven belong to the Lord your God. And yet he rejoiced in your fathers and loved them so much that he chose you, their children, to be above every other nation, as is evident today ... You must fear the Lord your God and worship him and cling to him, and take oaths by his name alone. He is your praise and he is your God, the one who has done mighty miracles you yourselves have seen." (Deuteronomy 10:12-15, 20-21, TLB)

Are you worshipping God with all your heart and soul? The Merriam Webster Dictionary (merriam-webster.com) defines worship like this: "the act of showing respect and love for a god especially by praying with other people who believe in the same god," "excessive admiration for someone," and "extravagant respect or admiration for or devotion to an object of esteem." I love that. "Extravagant respect or admiration for or devotion to" God. The definition of "praise" is: "to say or write good things about (someone or something)," "to express approval of (someone or something)," and "to glorify (a god or saint) especially by the attribution of perfections." How long has it been since you poured yourself out in prayer, praise, and worship, giving extravagant respect and admiration to the Lord your God? We simply cannot let our crammed-full schedules, activities, and even our good works steal from us the time to extravagantly honor God through our prayer, our praises, and our worship. Did you know that King David, the king of Israel God called a man after His own heart, worshipped the Lord with musical instruments, with dance, with songs, with poetry, and with prayer?

In 2 Samuel 6, David and the people of Israel went to retrieve the Ark of the Covenant, the only place in the Old Testament days where God/the Holy Spirit physically dwelt on earth at that time. (Today, we know God's Spirit lives in each person who accepts His salvation.) When they got the Ark, 2 Samuel 6:5 says, "David and all the Israelites were celebrating in the presence of the Lord. They were playing wooden instruments: lyres, harps, tambourines, rattles, and cymbals." Later, in verses 14-15 of the same chapter, David dances for the Lord: "Then David danced with all his might before the Lord. He had on a holy linen vest. David and all the Israelites shouted with joy and blew the trumpets as they brought the Ark of the Lord to the city." The Psalms are filled with praises to God written by David and his son Solomon. And Paul instructs us to worship and shows us his worship as an example many times in the books of the New Testament. Again and again throughout God's Word, we are commanded to give God praise, worship, honor, and glory. We were created to worship God, and when we do we get closer to Him than when we are doing anything else.

How do we worship? How do we praise? We know from David that we do these things "with all our might." Many verses instruct us to worship with singing, such as Judges 5:3 (KJV), which says, "Hear, O ye kings; give ear, O ye princes; I, even I, will sing unto the LORD; I will sing praise to the LORD God of Israel." Or how about 2 Samuel 22:50 (NIV), which says, "Therefore I will praise you, Lord, among the nations; I will sing the praises of your name." Consider Psalm 138:1-3 (MSG), which instructs us not only to sing, but also to thank God for all He has done. "Thank you! Everything in me says 'Thank you!' Angels listen as I sing my thanks. I kneel in worship facing your holy temple and say it again: 'Thank you! Thank you for your love, thank you for your faithfulness; Most holy is your name, most holy is your Word. The moment I called out, you stepped in; you made my life large with strength.'"

I love that interpretation right there: "You made my life large with strength." When I am at my weakest and I begin to praise, God can make my life large with strength. Just when I need it most. Don't get me wrong. We do not praise and worship God to get anything out of it for ourselves. Our motive should be to glorify God because He is worthy of being glorified. All day. Every day. But we do reap benefits when we glorify God with our praise and worship. We get covered with His love, raised up by His strength, comforted by His Spirit, drawn close in relationship with Christ. Wow! Let's get some worship on!

I personally love to use music to help me get into the frame of mind for worship. I have a worship channel on my television, and I often put it on in the background of my prayer, praise, and Bible study time. You can praise with Christian radio on in the car, sing at the top of your lungs whether you can keep a tune or not, or hum to yourself His praises. Your praise and worship time with the Lord should be as unique as you are. No one else can praise the Lord exactly like you can. I believe He is waiting to hear your voice of praise. I believe He rejoices in it, revels in it. I believe the angels are witness to your worship, and they worship with you. Worship becomes the bridge to Heaven, the entryway to the throne room of God.

Worship becomes the bridge to Heaven, the entryway to the throne room of God.

The combination of prayer, Bible study, and worship pack a one-two-three wallop to the devil. He cannot stand up to us if we put on the full armor of God and remain standing in His strength. These three acts transform you by the renewing of your mind, open your heart to receive all of God's blessings for you, and prepare you to do the "good works" God prepared for you. Ephesians 2:10 (AMP) puts it like this: "For we are His workmanship [His own master work, a work of art], created in Christ Jesus [reborn from above—spiritually transformed, renewed, ready to be used] for good works, which God prepared [for us] beforehand [taking paths which He set], so that we would walk in them [living the good life which He prearranged and made ready for us]."

Don't you love that? Are you ready to live the good life He prearranged and made ready for you? Even after the tragedy of losing Gavin, I know that I know that I know Jesus has a plan for the rest of my life. He has good things planned for me to do. He has birthed in me a new desire to reach others, share my story, and help them develop a foundation, find freedom, and live out a lifestyle of faith. It is a journey I will walk out for the rest of my days on this earth, because the alternative would be to give up, wallow in my pain and make no future for my family because of our loss. I refuse to give the devil anything else. I declare I will embrace faith as my lifestyle, covering myself with the Spirit of the Word of God, connecting to Christ with my prayers, and giving God all of my worship. Won't you join me?

Still in the Storm: Putting Your Armor On

1. How important is your prayer life to you? What does it look like?

   _____

   _____

   _____

   _____

   _____

   _____

2. What tools are you using to study the scriptures? What steps will you take to read and learn more?

   _____

   _____

   _____

   _____

   _____

   _____

3. What does praise and worship mean to you? How can you make your praise and worship more about God and His glory?

   _____

   _____

   _____

   _____

   _____

   _____

Still in the Storm: A Prayer of Praise

Dear Father In Jesus Name,

I thank you for life, and giving me life more abundantly. I am so thankful that today is a new day for my life. Your mercies for me are new every morning. Great is your faithfulness to me, Lord. I thank you Lord that as I praise you my spirit is strengthened, and I am renewed day after day from the inside out. No matter what happens in my day, I will praise you. I will praise you in the good times, and I will praise you in the hard times. I open my heart to you, and thank you for filling it with your power, strength, and love. As I praise you, I thank you that my faith is being built, and hope is being restored to me as I experience your love in my praise. As I praise you, I realize that I don't have to beg or plead for you to come close because you are always close, and your spirit is living in me. Thank you Lord that you are never distant from me. I open my heart, my mind, my will, and my life to you. Everything I am and everything I will be is only because of you. Help me to fully walk in a lifestyle of faith. I praise you for this day and everyday that I have your life flowing in me and through me.

In Jesus's precious name I pray,
Amen.

Put Your Armor On: The Next Steps

- Set for yourself some new prayer goals. Expand the ways you pray by trying new things, such as singing your prayers, drawing your prayer, or writing prayer and praise poetry. Change the scenery of where you pray by taking a walk outdoors, finding a quiet closet or corner to shut yourself away with God, or praying with others.

- Buy a new Bible with different features than you have used before. Grab some highlighters. Get out a pen. Try reading a new translation or picking up some Bible studies. You can do so many things with God's word. Choose one book of the Bible and look for repeated words. Write them down. See what God's main themes are in different books. Be intentional and disciplined in your Bible study time. You cannot afford for your sword to get rusty and dull.

- Ask the Holy Spirit to reveal the truths He wants you to see in the words you are reading. Consider joining a Bible study with others so you can learn together and hear others' revelations.

- Stream or download praise and worship music. Let music minister to your soul as you say out loud some words of praise, honor, and glory to God. At the beginning of your prayers, before any requests, glorify God. Tell Him how much you love Him. Think of all the good things He has done in your life and relive them with Him. Then be still and listen for His voice.

CHAPTER NINE: FELLOWSHIP, FAITH, AND THE FUTURE

*"The disciples just sat there, awed! 'Who is this,'
they asked themselves, 'that even the winds
and the sea obey him?'"*

– Matthew 8:27 (TLB)

At the time of this writing, my family is approaching the one-year mark since Gavin went to be with Jesus. One year of living out faith in a way we never experienced before. One year of staying in the boat with Jesus and holding on tighter to Him and each other than we had in the past. One year of finding a new normal and discovering what happens when you are "Still in the Storm." We chose this title for the book purposely because it has two meanings. Right now, we are still in the storm. In other words, we remain in the middle of it. It hasn't miraculously cleared up and gone away. It feels on many days like the dark clouds surround us, huge waves still break over our bow, and the rain cascades over us. Lightning crashes all around, and sometimes we wonder if we can stand the pain of this loss.

The second way to read this title is with the emphasis on being still. Utterly motionless. Allowing the storm to swirl around us while we remain upright and focused. When we stand still in the storm, we refuse to give the devil any ground. We do not give in to fear, to helplessness or hopelessness. We do not keel over in our grief or hand over our faith. We remain still, standing between the problem and the promises of God. We remain still because it is in the stillness that the Holy Spirit can speak to us, comfort us, encourage us. In short, in the stillness He keeps us breathing and moving forward. Sometimes the boat moves forward only a little. Sometimes it gets carried further from the shore. But little by little we are inching towards the other side. We know we will make it out of the boat and onto dry land. In order for our faith to take us into our future, we need to realize that as believers in Christ we are all in the boat together.

We experience the storms of life together. Not just Jeannie and me. But you and me. Your family and mine. Your church and mine. Your friends and mine. All of us who have accepted Jesus Christ as our Savior and who want to walk in the fullness of His grace are in this together. God calls us to live as one body, the Body of Christ. To live and work and fellowship and spread the gospel together. In Matthew's account of Jesus calming the storm, the disciples marvel at the miracle Christ performed. They experience awe together. They wonder together who Jesus was that He had such power. They sit in the boat together. They live through the storm together. Are you catching the theme here? They stick it out together.

I am sure you know the old expression "strength in numbers." The Bible confirms this throughout the text. Right after God finished creating the world and declaring that it was good, He looked down at Adam and saw that he was alone. He said that it was not good for Adam to be alone. He put Adam to sleep, removed one of his ribs, and created Eve to be Adam's companion, wife, and lover. God states in Genesis 2:18: "Then the LORD God said, 'It is not good that the man should be alone; I will make him a helper fit for him.'" Throughout God's Word, people are seen traveling, living, and worshipping together. Adam and Eve. Abraham and his brother Lot. Moses and his brother Aaron. David and his best friend Jonathan. Mary, Martha, and Lazarus. Jesus and the twelve disciples. To live out faith as our lifestyle under the biblical model, we have to do life with others. We need to walk out our faith journey in relationship with others. Others who are as imperfect, sinful, and selfish as we are. Others who are as forgiven, redeemed, and faith-filled as we are. We are all works in progress, and faith in fellowship with others can be hard. Still, it is suggested we do it.

126

Chapter Nine: Fellowship, Faith, and the Future

Ephesians 4:9-12 (ESV) says: "Two are better than one, because they have a good reward for their toil. For if they fall, one will lift up his fellow. But woe to him who is alone when he falls and has not another to lift him up! Again, if two lie together, they keep warm, but how can one keep warm alone? And though a man might prevail against one who is alone, two will withstand him—a threefold cord is not quickly broken." Think about the truth in that last line. If you have a piece of rope, it has strength. But it becomes stronger when you add another rope to it. If you get a third rope and braid the three together, the ability to bear weight and pull heavy objects is compounded. It is much more difficult to break a threefold cord than any of the individual ones.

Like rope, when two or more people gather together with the same faith, the same prayers, the same hope for the future, their ability to stand strong in the lifestyle of faith is compounded. It grows exponentially greater. As a bonus, Jesus promises, "For where two or three gather in my name, there am I with them" (Matthew 18:20, NIV). Not only do we find comfort and assurance and strength in each other, but Jesus promises to be right there with us. Let me tell you, it is a tall order to fellowship with other people when you don't feel like it. Maybe you have not found the "perfect" church where you feel like you fit. Maybe you have coworkers who get on your nerves at the office all day and the last thing you want to do in the evenings is connect with more people in a small group or Bible study or spend your weekend in church, smiling and shaking hands. Maybe you have been hurt or betrayed by people who claim to love Jesus. Believe me, I get it. Yet fellowship is critical to a lifestyle of faith. Even, sometimes especially, when you do not feel like it.

Jeannie and I did not feel like being around other people after Gavin died. It would have been much easier to curl up in our grief and stay in bed on Sunday mornings. Although it was usually unintentional on their parts, many people said hurtful things. The exact wrong things. Or avoided us altogether because they did not know what to say. Sometimes going to church and putting on the façade of, "Hey, how are you doing?" "Getting through, how are you?" felt overwhelmingly difficult. We had to be very intentional about spending time with people, about going to church, or else we would have become hermits!

When our hearts are hurting or our faith has hit a rough patch, spending time with others who are like-minded is really important. People are not our source; Jesus is. But people who try to live out biblical principles and who care about us, can love on us, serve us, and take care of us in the best way they know how when we let them in. Not long after Gavin passed away, my wife decided to invite a group of ladies into our home for a Bible study. That was not an easy thing for her to do, but the Lord put it on her heart to have six or seven ladies into our home for an eight-week study. Jeannie reached out and brought people into her world. When she did, she found connection. She found healing in learning and serving, as she and the women studied together and did outreaches like filling shoeboxes for Operation Christmas Child.

Jeannie is not Superwoman. She may not have felt like putting herself out there just a couple of months after Gavin's death. But she is obedient and faith-filled. She knows God's Word tells us to fellowship. She knows the importance of corporate prayer and praise. So she steeled herself and stepped out in her faith. God rewarded her efforts with some real heart connections, some bits of light in the darkness of our loss, and friendships that remain today. This special group of women plan to continue studying and growing in their faith together.

Check out Hebrews 10:24-25 (NIV), which says, "And let us consider how we may spur one another on toward love and good deeds, not giving up meeting together, as some are in the habit of doing, but encouraging one another—and all the more as you see the Day approaching." The Day spoken of here is the day that Jesus returns to the earth. Until then, we are charged with gathering together. What are the kinds of things we are to do together? Live, laugh, and learn. Eat, encourage, praise, and pray. Help each other. Serve each other. Love in a way that impresses others who do not know Jesus. Forgive and keep peace with each other in ways that draw the attention of the rest of the world.

Here are a few of the ways we are to fellowship together, according to God's Word:

Ephesians 5:19 (NCV) says, "Speak to each other with psalms, hymns, and spiritual songs, singing and making music in your hearts to the Lord."

Colossians 3:16: "Let the message of Christ dwell among you richly as you teach and admonish one another with all wisdom through psalms, hymns, and songs from the Spirit, singing to God with gratitude in your hearts."

James 5:16 (NKJV): "Confess your trespasses to one another, and pray for one another, that you may be healed. The effective, fervent prayer of a righteous man avails much."

Acts 1:14 (NLT): "They all met together and were constantly united in prayer, along with Mary the mother of Jesus, several other women, and the brothers of Jesus."

Acts 2:42 (MSG): "They committed themselves to the teaching of the apostles, the life together, the common meal, and the prayers."

1 Corinthians 12:12 (NKJV): "For as the body is one and has many members, but all the members of that one body, being many, are one body, so also is Christ."

1 Peter 4:8-10 (NLT): "Most important of all, continue to show deep love for each other, for love covers a multitude of sins. Cheerfully share your home with those who need a meal or a

place to stay. God has given each of you a gift from his great variety of spiritual gifts. Use them well to serve one another."

From these verses, what are we to do in fellowship with others? Eat together, open our homes to each other, share our spiritual gifts by serving each other, admonish each other with wisdom, sing together, confess our sins to each other, and pray for each other. These are just a few of the many benefits of fellowship.Living life together can be tough – personalities sometimes clash, selfishness rears its ugly head – but even the conflicts can be learning experiences that grow and mature our faith. We learn to overlook imperfections. With love, we strive to hold each other accountable. We walk out forgiveness. We learn to resolve conflict. We work together towards common goals of loving better, going deeper, and drawing others to Christ.

How do you heal when people say the wrong things, do the wrong things, or hurt your feelings? With determination. With discipline. By pressing in to the Holy Spirit and His comfort more than ever before. Now, I am not saying you have to be best friends with everybody. Jesus picked only twelve men to travel with Him and be His closest friends. Jeannie and I are very selective in who we spend time with. We don't go around with everybody. We need to become intimate with a few like-minded people who won't shy away from our pain but will sit with us in it. Those who will join us in being still in our storm.

When we develop that close network, we see grace and love in action. Meals arrive, childcare is arranged, and true friends are just there when their presence is needed. I seek counsel and fellowship with pastors who have spoken into my life and mentored me. I share confidences, seek advice, and allow these few men to come into my pain. They pray for and with me, listen to me, and offer words of encouragement. When you have other trustworthy believers in your boat, they hold up umbrellas of protection. They fill buckets and bail when your boat starts taking on water.

Chapter Nine: Fellowship, Faith, and the Future

If you are not in fellowship with other Christ-followers, you are missing a big part of faith as your lifestyle. I encourage you to connect in a Bible study group, a men's fellowship group, a church, a small group, or other gathering of believers on a regular basis. At least once a week. Aim to develop a few close friendships if you don't already have them. Find a few trustworthy friends you can share all your good, bad, and ugly with. As your friendship stands the test of time, these close relationships will become some of your greatest treasures.

I can hear some of you saying, "Jamey, you mean I have to go to church to be a Christian?" No, you do not have to go to church to be a Christian. You can love Jesus and live for Him without going to church every Sunday. But let me ask you this: why wouldn't you want to spend time with Jesus in His house with others who follow Him? I believe the devil gets the best opportunities to attack us when we become isolated. Think of any predator looking for prey. What is the first thing the predator tries to do? Identify any animal that might be vulnerable, then separate it from the rest of its kind.

When you experience suffering, you are weak. You are vulnerable. The last thing you need to be is isolated. Instead, spend time with God's people regularly, no matter how wildly your emotions are swinging. Corporate worship rebuilds your broken heart. Corporate prayer assures you God is with you, among you, right in the middle of your pain. Corporate teaching cuts through the dark emotions with wisdom, and corporate gatherings surround you and keep you from becoming isolated, the perfect prey for the devil's attacks.

* * *

I titled this chapter "Faith, Fellowship, and the Future" to complete our journey of faith in the boat. To get to the other side of my story. To help you get to the other side of yours by living a journey of faith as your foundation, your freedom, and your lifestyle. Together as one body in Christ, we can stand still in any storm. I believe it with everything in me. Now more than ever.

Jesus loved me and you so much that He decided to die for us rather than live without us. So it's time for us to get in the boat and sail with Him, whether we encounter stormy seas that threaten to toss into oblivion or the calmest, clearest waters we've ever known. Chances are very good that in this life you will experience both. If you trust in Jesus enough to get in the boat with Him, you have to trust Him enough to stay in it when the waves get rough.

After all, the alternative of jumping out of the boat into those rough waters isn't any more appealing, is it? Watch what God can do with your pain. Hang in there when you feel seasick and see what He can put together from a life pounded by rain and waves. God creates masterpieces from broken pieces.

God creates masterpieces from broken pieces.

I am a living testimony to that fact. God can turn your suffering into your greatest success. That's where the faith lifestyle fits. Immersing yourself in prayer, praise, God's Word, and God's people is like wrapping a great, big soft blanket around yourself on a dark, cold night.

Remember what Joseph said in Genesis 50:20 (NLT)? "You intended to harm me, but God intended it all for good. He brought me to this position so I could save the lives of many people." That brings us to the wrap-up of the purpose of our faith lifestyle.

What is all this faith for? Why do we need it, beyond the hope it gives us? Why is it so important that we cloak ourselves, steep ourselves, in all of these faith-building tools? As Joseph puts it, so you can save the lives of many people. Me? You might be saying. Yes. You.

Your faith will draw others to you. They will see a difference. They will see your peace in the storms of life. The human spirit longs for that peace, for connection, for relationship. They need Jesus more than ever today, and it is getting harder and harder to find Him as our culture drifts further and further from Him.

After Jesus's resurrection from the dead, the disciples went to the mountain in Galilee where Jesus had instructed them before His death to go. There, it says in Matthew 28, Jesus appeared to them, and that's where He gave them the purpose for discipleship. The reason they had followed Christ as He taught forgiveness, healed the sick, fought the authority of the day, and died on the cross. In Matthew 28:18-20 (NIV), it states: "Then Jesus came to them and said, 'All authority in heaven and on earth has been given to me. Therefore go and make disciples of all nations, baptizing them in the name of the Father and of the Son and of the Holy Spirit, and teaching them to obey everything I have commanded you. And surely I am with you always, to the very end of the age.'"

Christ lives in us, dwells among us, guides and keeps us, so we can help others get to know Him. So we can bring others into the body of Christ. So we can make disciples of all the nations, teaching them how faith can be their foundation, their freedom, and the greatest lifestyle they have ever known. That's how Jesus brings success out of your suffering, passion and purpose from your pain. He never wastes a moment, a feeling, a circumstance. He can turn everything that has happened to you, everything meant for evil against you, into the greatest good.

Will you still feel pain? Absolutely. I will never "get over" my son's death. Gavin will always be part of the fabric of my life's story. To pull out the thread of pain and grief would be to unravel the whole beautiful tapestry Christ is weaving from my life. You need the dark colors to contrast the bright. But the lifestyle of faith means understanding that even in the middle of every storm, you are in right standing with God. You don't have to do anything more to obtain what you know you already have. When you feel confused or in pain, pray and ask God for peace and you already have it.

Through prayer, through speaking what you believe out loud, you can ask God for peace and He will give it to you. You speak it out so you can hear it. Faith comes by hearing, and hearing by the Word of God, so when you speak out the Word of God, you allow faith to come in that moment. It transforms your mind.

When Jesus said, "It is finished" as he died on the cross, he did not mean His life was over. No, he was saying his work was finished. Because of His finished work on the cross we now can come boldly before the throne of God and have instant access to Him. How? By Faith!

That is a faith lifestyle that's contagious. That's the kind of disciples we want to be. This is what works in my life. My faith and hope are restored by His finished work, by His genuine love extended towards all of us. What a gift! How exciting it is to be perfected through Christ. I believe, I believe, I believe. Don't you? And by believing in this life-changing, life-saving gift and telling others all about it, we can change the world. For eternity.

* * *

That's what gives me renewed passion and purpose to go on. That's what gives me glimpses of the "hope and future" God's Word promises in Jeremiah 33:3. Even in the middle of Gavin's fight against cancer and in all the months since his death, we could see glimpses of our future through our faith. When ICU doctors asked us how we were keeping such assurance and peace, we had the opportunity to share that faith. When a pro basketball player was so touched by Gavin's story that he wore Gavin's name on his game shoes, we saw God moving. When pastors around the country ask me to speak on faith at revivals, conferences, and services, I can feel God restoring and reassuring me. When God spoke to me in my brown leather recliner shortly after Gavin's death and birthed in me a dream to grow others' faith through a new ministry called Faith Builders International, we could see Him weaving purpose through our pain. When

I see my son Preston engaging with God more deeply than he did before losing his brother, I see faith in action for our future.

Our future now includes loving a little more fiercely, valuing our family time more than ever, praying more deeply as husband and wife, studying more of God's Word together, and making plans to share these vital faith-building tools with everyone God puts in our path. I can see the fingerprints of God all over Faith Builders International. I see the potential victory of using our influence to tell others about Christ. I have been able to reach more unchurched people in the past twelve months through Gavin's story than I have in my whole ministry. So even though Gavin's story did not have the fairytale "happy ending" in this life, his life had purpose. It had meaning. And God is still using it to affect the hearts and spirits of many. His life's impact for the kingdom of God has just begun.

Back in the summer of 2011, I was driving some back roads of Kansas on my way to speak at a church. While driving, I began to get a download on what God wanted me to do. The Lord planted the seeds for this faith ministry back then. I just didn't know when those seeds would take root and push through the soil. On that drive, the Lord ministered to me in such a way that in my heart I heard these words: "I want you to build people's faith in me, restore those who are hurting with my hope, and extend my genuine love so all would know I am real."

It was in that moment that the ministry of Faith Builders International was first birthed in my heart. I thought, "This has to be from God. I am not remotely looking to start a ministry." I had been in church ministry for a number of years, and in 2011 I was working as a businessman. Quite honestly, I wasn't looking to get back into ministry anytime soon. I was running my own business, and that alone was keeping me very busy. While the idea began to germinate in my heart, I knew it was not the right season. The seeds remained dormant for the next four years.

Two weeks after Gavin's death, the new life contained within those seeds broke through. I wasn't looking to add more to my plate but I knew that even in tragedy God can always triumph, and I believe that Faith

Builders International will touch the world and His Church with His tangible presence, power, and love.

Today, Faith Builders International is fully committed to serve everyone we come in contact with, by expressing the authentic message of Jesus Christ. It is our goal to share this gospel message of Jesus to a world that is hurting, lost, broken, and in desperate need of God to save, heal, deliver, and restore it. When people ask me and Jeannie how I can do this, start a ministry and speak and preach about my young son's death, I tell them it is because I am certain I will see my son again. We will be reunited in Heaven. It's just a matter of time. In the meantime, while I am still on earth, I have a job to do, a responsibility to those I meet to share with them the best gift I have ever received – my salvation, the unconditional love of a Savior, and peace that passes all understanding.

The storm of losing Gavin could have capsized my boat. It could have thrown me into the raging seas. But Jesus was in the boat with me. He never left my side. He calmed the storm inside me that came with Gavin's death, and now I see new life coming through. I know I made it to the other side. While I still would not choose to go through the storm of losing my son, I can now see how life is sustained and grows when waters are stirred. When water stands still and becomes stagnant, everything in it dies. Moving water equals living water. And living water is what Jesus promises, a metaphor for the life He gives ... life more abundantly. Life filled with love, joy, peace, patience, kindness, goodness, gentleness, faithfulness, and self-control. Life filled with peace, passion, and purpose. Life that never ends.

John 4:13-14 says, "Jesus answered, 'Everyone who drinks this water will be thirsty again, but whoever drinks the water I give them will never thirst. Indeed, the water I give them will become in them a spring of water welling up to eternal life.'"

Chapter Nine: Fellowship, Faith, and the Future

One year after Gavin's death, I grieve with hope. I wake in the mornings filled with purpose. I rely on my faith. I look forward to seeing God's plans unfold in Faith Builders. I get excited when Gavin's story makes a difference in people's lives. I can't wait until I see my son again. In the meantime, I will stay still in the storm.

Close your eyes. Picture yourself standing in a boat, dark clouds swirling around you, lightning crashing far too close, waves breaking over the bow as you take on water. You are scared, cold, and really wet. Now picture Jesus sleeping in the stern. You lean over, careful not to overturn your craft, and shake His shoulder. He wakes instantly and looks deeply into your eyes. You know He registers the fear in them, sees your shaking body. His face fills with compassion. Christ lifts a hand and firmly tells the storm to stop.

Suddenly, the clouds roll back. The lightning ceases. Brilliant streaks of sunlight break through the clouds. You feel the warmth on your skin. The rain stops completely and the calm seas are as smooth as glass. You look down to see that you are all in one piece. Still dripping wet, still a little shaky. But your Savior is with you. He never left your side. Suddenly, Jesus draws His arm in a wide arc above His head, and the sky fills with the bright colors of a rainbow. His promise.

Together, you and Jesus remained still in the storm. And you always will. With faith as your foundation, your freedom, and your lifestyle, you can be assured that no matter what circumstance may try to topple you, you will make it to the other side.

Still in the Storm: Fellowship, Faith and Your Future

1. In what ways are you "plugged in" to your Church?

   _____

   _____

   _____

   _____

   _____

   _____

2. How has your faith grown through the reading of this book? What specific things will you do to continue to make faith your lifestyle?

   _____

   _____

   _____

   _____

   _____

   _____

3. What plans can you see that the Lord has for you to give you a "hope and a future"? What beauty can you see springing up from the ashes of your past or present circumstances?

   _____

   _____

   _____

   _____

   _____

   _____

Still in the Storm: A Prayer for My Future

Dear Father in Jesus Name,

    I thank you that through the storms of life you cause me to be still and know you are God. I thank you that when Jesus said "It Is Finished" that his life wasn't over, but his work was done and I was made righteous through him. I realize more and more that you are with me in every season of life. I thank you for placing the right people in my life at the right time to help propel me into the purpose you have for my life. As I continue to study your word I thank you that my faith grows. I am so blessed and thankful that your love is unconditional and that you are always for me, and never against me. I thank you for strength to stand in the face of adversity, and by faith I see my victory on the other side. I know I do not have to strive to be or do anything more for you to love me. I am enough for you. I praise you for bringing beauty from the ashes in my life. I love you, Jesus. Thank you for your perfect, finished work on the cross.

In your precious name I pray,
Amen.

Faith, Fellowship, and the Future: The Next Steps

- If you are not part of a church, find one! If you go to church but do not regularly "do life" with other Christ-followers, make it a priority to join a small group, a weekly Bible study, a prayer group, a men's or women's ministry, or other small gathering of people you can trust and become intimate with. Don't put it off. Do it this week!

- Ask the Holy Spirit to help you be more open, honest, and vulnerable with a few trusted friends. Ask them if they see you standing still in the storm? Ask them to pray with you and for you, and be specific about your needs. Let others serve you when you need to be served. Don't let pride keep you from receiving the gift of blessings from God's people. If you have a financial need, share it with your close-knit group. If you need meals, let your congregation know. There are times when you serve in the body of Christ, and times in life when you need to allow the body to serve you.

- Do some vision casting, some fasting and praying, and goal planning. Write down what you believe God is calling you to next. What is springing up from the ashes of your circumstances? What is He asking you to do right now to bring those visions and goals to fruition? Ask the Lord for boldness to share about Him, strength to carry the burden of grief, and any other "tools" you need for the mission He is giving you. He will be faithful to provide them.

CHAPTER TEN: FAITH PROMISES FROM GOD'S WORD

Through these he gave us the very great and precious promises. With these gifts you can share in God's nature, and the world will not ruin you with its evil desires.

- 2 Peter 1:4, NCV

Throughout this book, I have quoted lots of Scriptures to help reveal the many ways God's Word can build our faith, teach us to trust in Him, and grow us. The Bible is God's love letter to us, and it is packed with promises to comfort and encourage us as we remain still in the storm.

Here are a few of the many verses that have helped sustain my family during our time of grief. Some are promises I have known since I was a teen. Some are precious verses I discovered in my ministry years before losing Gavin. Some are new favorites I return to again and again when feelings of grief threaten to overwhelm me. Many of these verses I cling to on a regular basis to sustain me as I walk out my new normal without my son.

While this chapter in no way is meant to replace your daily study of the Word, it does contain important verses to strengthen you as you walk out whatever path the Lord has you on right now. You can use this quick guide to help you whenever you need it. Keep it handy. Write key verses down in your own prayer or study journal or on notecards you can tuck places where you will find them and see them when you need them most.

Let the voice of God through His holy Word be the healing ointment on the open wounds of your soul.

For comfort and encouragement, turn frequently and fervently to the book of Psalms. King David was called "a man after God's own heart," but this king knew plenty of persecution, sorrow, and sin. The collection of poetry, songs, and cries from the heart to God that we know as Psalms soothes the same wounded places in our hearts and souls today. Proverbs teaches us about wisdom and right ways to live. And the various books of the New Testament strengthen us in our knowledge of Jesus, the Holy Spirit, His teachings, and how we are to live on this earth and draw others to a knowledge and love of Jesus Christ. Here is a sampling, by category, to get you started on your own Scripture journey:

COMFORT

Joshua 1:9 (NCV): Remember that I commanded you to be strong and brave. Don't be afraid, because the Lord your God will be with you everywhere you go.

Psalm 23:4 (TLB): Even when walking through the dark valley of death I will not be afraid, for you are close beside me, guarding, guiding all the way.

Psalm 27:1 (NLT): The Lord is my light and my salvation—so why should I be afraid? The Lord is my fortress, protecting me from danger, so why should I tremble?

Psalm 34:18 (NIV): The Lord is close to the brokenhearted and saves those who are crushed in spirit.

Psalm 56:8 (NLT): You keep track of all my sorrows. You have collected all my tears in your bottle. You have recorded each one in your book.

Psalm 63:1 (TLB): O God, my God! How I search for you! How I thirst for you in this parched and weary land where there is no water. How I long to find you!

Psalm 86:17 (NIV): Give me a sign of your goodness, that my enemies may see it and be put to shame, for you, LORD, have helped me and comforted me.

Psalm 139:1-4 (NLT): O LORD, you have examined my heart and know everything about me. You know when I sit down or stand up. You know my thoughts even when I'm far away. You see me when I travel and when I rest at home. You know everything I do. You know what I am going to say even before I say it, LORD.

Psalm 139:16 (NLT): Every day of my life was recorded in your book. Every moment was laid out before a single day had passed.

Isaiah 61:3 (KJV): To appoint unto them that mourn in Zion, to give unto them beauty for ashes, the oil of joy for mourning, the garment of praise for the spirit of heaviness; that they might be called trees of righteousness, the planting of the LORD, that he might be glorified.

2 Corinthians 1:3-4 (NIV): Praise be to the God and Father of our Lord Jesus Christ, the Father of compassion and the God of all comfort, who comforts us in all our troubles, so that we can comfort those in any trouble with the comfort we ourselves receive from God.

ENCOURAGEMENT

Psalm 46:1-3 (ESV): God is our refuge and strength, a very present help in trouble. Therefore we will not fear though the earth gives way, though the mountains be moved into the heart of the sea, though its waters roar and foam, though the mountains tremble at its swelling.

Proverbs 3:5-6 (TLB): If you want favor with both God and man, and a reputation for good judgment and common sense, then trust the Lord completely; don't ever trust yourself. In everything you do, put God first, and he will direct you and crown your efforts with success.

Isaiah 41:10 (NCV): So don't worry, because I am with you. Don't be afraid, because I am your God. I will make you strong and will help you; I will support you with my right hand that saves you.

Zephaniah 3:17 (NIV): The Lord your God is with you, the Mighty Warrior who saves. He will take great delight in you; in his love he will no longer rebuke you, but will rejoice over you with singing.

Romans 8:28 (NLT): And we know that God causes everything to work together for the good of those who love God and are called according to his purpose for them.

Romans 8:31 (KJV): What shall we then say to these things? If God be for us, who can be against us?

Romans 12:10-12 (ESV): Love one another with brotherly affection. Outdo one another in showing honor. Do not be slothful in zeal, be fervent in spirit, serve the Lord. Rejoice in hope, be patient in tribulation, be constant in prayer.

Ephesians 2:10 (AMP): For we are His workmanship [His own master work, a work of art], created in Christ Jesus [reborn from above—spiritually transformed, renewed, ready to be used] for good works, which God prepared [for us] beforehand [taking paths which He set], so that we would walk in them [living the good life which He prearranged and made ready for us].

James 4:8 (NKJV): Draw near to God and He will draw near to you.

ETERNITY

Psalm 90:2 (KJV): Before the mountains were brought forth, or ever thou hadst formed the earth and the world, even from everlasting to everlasting, thou art God.

1 Corinthians 15:54-55 (NLT): Then, when our dying bodies have been transformed into bodies that will never die, this Scripture will be fulfilled: "Death is swallowed up in victory. O death, where is your victory? O death, where is your sting?"

2 Corinthians 3:6 (NLT): The old written covenant ends in death; but under the new covenant, the Spirit gives life.

2 Corinthians 4:16-18 (NKJV): Therefore we do not lose heart. Even though our outward man is perishing, yet the inward man is being renewed day by day. For our light affliction, which is but for a moment, is working for us a far more exceeding and eternal weight of glory, while we do not look at the things which are seen, but at the things which are not seen. For the things which are seen are temporary, but the things which are not seen are eternal.

Hebrews 13:8 (NLT): Jesus Christ is the same yesterday, today, and forever.

FAITH

John 11:40 (NASB): Jesus said to her, "Did I not say to you that if you believe, you will see the glory of God?"

Romans 10:17 (NKJV): So then faith comes by hearing, and hearing by the word of God.

2 Corinthians 5:6-7 (NIV): Therefore we are always confident and know that as long as we are at home in the body we are away from the Lord. For we live by faith, not by sight.

Galatians 2:20 (NIV): I have been crucified with Christ and I no longer live, but Christ lives in me. The life I now live in the body, I live by faith in the Son of God, who loved me and gave himself for me.

Hebrews 11:1 (KJV): Now faith is the substance of things hoped for, the evidence of things not seen.

Hebrews 12:1-2 (KJV): Lay aside every weight, and the sin which doth so easily beset us, and let us run with patience the race that is set before us, looking unto Jesus the author and finisher of our faith; who for the joy that was set before him endured the cross, despising the shame, and is set down at the right hand of the throne of God.

FELLOWSHIP

Genesis 2:18 (ESV): Then the LORD God said, "It is not good that the man should be alone; I will make him a helper fit for him."

Ephesians 4:9-12 (ESV): Two are better than one, because they have a good reward for their toil. For if they fall, one will lift up his fellow. But woe to him who is alone when he falls and has not another to lift him up! Again, if two lie together, they keep warm, but how can one keep warm alone? And though a man might prevail against one who is alone, two will withstand him—a threefold cord is not quickly broken.

FREEDOM

John 8:36 (NKJV): Therefore if the Son makes you free, you shall be free indeed.

Romans 8:2 (NLT): And because you belong to him, the power of the life-giving Spirit has freed you from the power of sin that leads to death.

2 Corinthians 3:17 (NIV): Now the Lord is the Spirit, and where the Spirit of the Lord is, there is freedom.

Galatians 5:1 (NIV): It is for freedom that Christ has set us free. Stand firm, then, and do not let yourselves be burdened again by a yoke of slavery.

Galatians 5:13 (ESV): For you were called to freedom, brothers. Only do not use your freedom as an opportunity for the flesh, but through love serve one another.

1 Peter 2:16-17 (NLT): For you are free, yet you are God's slaves, so don't use your freedom as an excuse to do evil. Respect everyone, and love the family of believers.

<u>GRACE</u>

Romans 3:23-24 (NASB): for all have sinned and fall short of the glory of God, being justified as a gift by His grace through the redemption which is in Christ Jesus.

Ephesians 1:7 (NIV): In him we have redemption through his blood, the forgiveness of sins, in accordance with the riches of God's grace.

Ephesians 2:8 (NIV): For it is by grace you have been saved, through faith--and this is not from yourselves, it is the gift of God.

Ephesians 4:7 (NKJV): But to each one of us grace was given according to the measure of Christ's gift.

2 Corinthians 12:8-9 (NCV): I begged the Lord three times to take this problem away from me. But he said to me, "My grace is enough for you. When you are weak, my power is made perfect in you." So I am very happy to brag about my weaknesses. Then Christ's power can live in me.

2 Timothy 2:1 (NKJV): You therefore, my son, be strong in the grace that is in Christ Jesus.

Titus 2:11 (NCV): That is the way we should live, because God's grace that can save everyone has come.

HEALING

Proverbs 4:20-22 (NLT): My child, pay attention to what I say. Listen carefully to my words. Don't lose sight of them. Let them penetrate deep into your heart, for they bring life to those who find them, and healing to their whole body.

Isaiah 53:5 (NCV): But he was wounded for the wrong we did; he was crushed for the evil we did. The punishment, which made us well, was given to him, and we are healed because of his wounds.

Mark 5:34 (NKJV): And He said to her, "Daughter, your faith has made you well. Go in peace, and be healed of your affliction."

Mark 10:52 (NIV): "Go," said Jesus, "your faith has healed you." Immediately he received his sight and followed Jesus along the road.

HOLY SPIRIT

Psalm 104:30 (TLB): Then you send your Spirit, and new life is born to replenish all the living of the earth.

John 14:16-17 (KJV): And I will pray the Father, and he shall give you another Comforter, that he may abide with you for ever; Even the Spirit of truth; whom the world cannot receive, because it seeth him not, neither knoweth him: but ye know him; for he dwelleth with you, and shall be in you.

John 14:26 (AMP): But the Helper (Comforter, Advocate, Intercessor—Counselor, Strengthener, Standby), the Holy Spirit, whom the Father will send in My name [in My place, to represent Me and act on My behalf], He will teach you all things. And He will help you remember everything that I have told you.

Acts 2:3-4 (NIV): They saw what seemed to be tongues of fire that separated and came to rest on each of them. All of them were filled with the Holy Spirit and began to speak in other tongues as the Spirit enabled them.

Romans 8:6 (NIV): The mind governed by the flesh is death, but the mind governed by the Spirit is life and peace.

1 Corinthians 6:17(a) (NIV): But whoever is united with the Lord is one with him in spirit.

Galatians 4:6 (NIV): Because you are his sons, God sent the Spirit of his Son into our hearts, the Spirit who calls out, "Abba, Father."

Galatians 5:22-23 (NLT): But the Holy Spirit produces this kind of fruit in our lives: love, joy, peace, patience, kindness, goodness, faithfulness, gentleness, and self-control. There is no law against these things!

2 Timothy 1:7 (NIV): For the Spirit God gave us does not make us timid, but gives us power, love and self-discipline.

LOVE

1 Chronicles 16:34 (NIV): Give thanks to the Lord, for he is good; his love endures forever.

Psalm 32:10 (NLT): Many sorrows come to the wicked, but unfailing love surrounds those who trust the Lord.

Jeremiah 31:3 (NIV): The Lord appeared to us in the past, saying: "I have loved you with an everlasting love; I have drawn you with unfailing kindness.

Romans 5:5 (NLT): For we know how dearly God loves us, because he has given us the Holy Spirit to fill our hearts with his love.

1 Corinthians 13: 1-8 (MSG): If I speak with human eloquence and angelic ecstasy but don't love, I'm nothing but the creaking of a rusty gate. If I speak God's Word with power, revealing all his mysteries and making everything plain as day, and if I have faith that says to a mountain, "Jump," and it jumps, but I don't love, I'm nothing. If I give everything I own to the poor and even go to the stake to be burned as a martyr, but I don't love, I've gotten nowhere. So, no matter what I say, what I believe, and what I do, I'm bankrupt without love.

Love never gives up.

Love cares more for others than for self.

Love doesn't want what it doesn't have.

Love doesn't strut,

Doesn't have a swelled head,

Doesn't force itself on others,

Isn't always "me first,"

Doesn't fly off the handle,

Doesn't keep score of the sins of others,

Doesn't revel when others grovel,

Takes pleasure in the flowering of truth,

Puts up with anything,

Trusts God always,

Always looks for the best,

Never looks back,

But keeps going to the end.

Love never dies.

1 Corinthians 13:13 (NCV): So these three things continue forever: faith, hope, and love. And the greatest of these is love.

1 John 4:16 (NIV): And so we know and rely on the love God has for us. God is love. Whoever lives in love lives in God, and God in them.

1 John 4:18 (NIV): There is no fear in love. But perfect love drives out fear, because fear has to do with punishment. The one who fears is not made perfect in love.

NEW LIFE

Psalm 118:14 (NIV): The Lord is my strength and my defense; he has become my salvation.

John 3:16 (KJV): For God so loved the world, that he gave his only begotten son, that whosoever believeth in him should not perish, but have everlasting life.

John 10:10 (AMP): The thief comes only in order to steal and kill and destroy. I came that they may have and enjoy life, and have it in abundance [to the full, till it overflows].

2 Corinthians 5:17-18 (NLT): This means that anyone who belongs to Christ has become a new person. The old life is gone; a new life has begun! And all of this is a gift from God, who brought us back to himself through Christ.

Galatians 3:13 (NLT): But Christ has rescued us from the curse pronounced by the law. When he was hung on the cross, he took upon himself the curse for our wrongdoing. For it is written in the Scriptures, "Cursed is everyone who is hung on a tree."

Colossians 3:1-3 (NIV): Since, then, you have been raised with Christ, set your hearts on things above, where Christ is, seated at the right hand of

God. Set your minds on things above, not on earthly things. For you died, and your life is now hidden with Christ in God.

John 1:12 (NIV): Yet to all who did receive him, to those who believed in his name, he gave the right to become children of God.

PEACE

Psalm 46:10 (NIV): Be still and know that I am God.

Isaiah 26:3 (NLT): You will keep in perfect peace all who trust in you, all whose thoughts are fixed on you!

Mark 4:39 (KJV): And he arose, and rebuked the wind, and said unto the sea, "Peace, be still." And the wind ceased, and there was a great calm.

John 14:27 (NKJV): Peace I leave with you. My peace I give to you; not as the world gives do I give to you. Let not your heart be troubled, neither let it be afraid.

John 16:33 (NLT): I have told you all this so that you may have peace in me. Here on earth you will have many trials and sorrows. But take heart, because I have overcome the world.

Philippians 4:7 (NKJV): And the peace of God, which surpasses all understanding, will guard your hearts and minds through Christ Jesus.

Hebrews 4:16 (NASB): Therefore let us draw near with confidence to the throne of grace, so that we may receive mercy and find grace to help in time of need.

2 Peter 1:2 (MSG): Grace and peace to you many times over as you deepen in your experience with God and Jesus, our Master.

PRAYER

Psalm 4:1 (NIV): Answer me when I call to you, my righteous God. Give me relief from my distress; have mercy on me and hear my prayer.

Psalm 145:18 (RSV): The Lord is near to all who call upon him, to all who call upon him in truth.

Jeremiah 29:12 (AMP): Then you will call on Me and you will come and pray to Me, and I will hear [your voice] and I will listen to you.

Mark 11:24 (NCV): Therefore I say to you, all things for which you pray and ask, believe that you have received them, and they will be granted you.

Luke 18:1 (NCV): Then Jesus used this story to teach his followers that they should always pray and never lose hope.

Philippians 4:6 (TLB): Don't worry about anything; instead, pray about everything; tell God your needs, and don't forget to thank him for his answers.

Colossians 4:2 (NKJV): Continue earnestly in prayer, being vigilant in it with thanksgiving;

1 Thessalonians 5:17 (NKJV): Pray without ceasing.

James 1:5-8 (MSG): If you don't know what you're doing, pray to the Father. He loves to help. You'll get his help, and won't be condescended to when you ask for it. Ask boldly, believingly, without a second thought. People who "worry their prayers" are like wind-whipped waves. Don't think you're going to get anything from the Master that way, adrift at sea, keeping all your options open.

1 John 5:14 (NIV): This is the confidence we have in approaching God: that if we ask anything according to his will, he hears us.

<u>REST</u>

Genesis 2:2-3 (NLT): On the seventh day God had finished his work of creation, so he rested from all his work. And God blessed the seventh day and declared it holy, because it was the day when he rested from all his work of creation.

Psalm 37:7 (TLB): Rest in the Lord; wait patiently for him to act. Don't be envious of evil men who prosper.

Psalm 127:2 (NKJV): It is vain for you to rise up early, To sit up late, To eat the bread of sorrows; For so He gives His beloved sleep.

Jeremiah 6:16 (NCV): This is what the Lord says: "Stand where the roads cross and look. Ask where the old way is, where the good way is, and walk on it. If you do, you will find rest for yourselves.

Jeremiah 31:2 (NIV): This is what the Lord says: "The people who survive the sword will find favor in the wilderness; I will come to give rest to Israel."

Matthew 11:28-30 (MSG): Are you tired? Worn out? Burned out on religion? Come to me. Get away with me and you'll recover your life. I'll show you how to take a real rest. Walk with me and work with me—watch how I do it. Learn the unforced rhythms of grace. I won't lay anything heavy or ill-fitting on you. Keep company with me and you'll learn to live freely and lightly."

Revelation 14:13 (NLT): And I heard a voice from heaven saying, "Write this down: Blessed are those who die in the Lord from now on. Yes, says the Spirit, they are blessed indeed, for they will rest from their hard work; for their good deeds follow them!"

STRENGTH

Deuteronomy 31:6 (NIV): Be strong and courageous. Do not be afraid or terrified because of them, for the LORD your God goes with you; he will never leave you nor forsake you.

Psalm 16:8 (NIV): I keep my eyes always on the Lord. With him at my right hand, I will not be shaken.

Psalm 73:26 (NCV): My body and my mind may become weak, but God is my strength. He is mine forever.

Isaiah 41:10 (ESV): Fear not, for I am with you; be not dismayed, for I am your God; I will strengthen you, I will help you, I will uphold you with my righteous right hand.

Joshua 1:9 (NCV): Remember that I commanded you to be strong and brave. Don't be afraid, because the Lord your God will be with you every-where you go.

Romans 8:26 (ESV): Likewise the Spirit helps us in our weakness. For we do not know what to pray for as we ought, but the Spirit himself intercedes for us with groanings too deep for words.

Ephesians 6:10-18 (NCV): Finally, be strong in the Lord and in his great power. Put on the full armor of God so that you can fight against the devil's evil tricks. Our fight is not against people on earth but against the rulers and authorities and the powers of this world's darkness, against the spiri-tual powers of evil in the heavenly world. That is why you need to put on God's full armor. Then on the day of evil you will be able to stand strong. And when you have finished the whole fight, you will still be standing. So stand strong, with the belt of truth tied around your waist and the pro-tection of right living on your chest. On your feet wear the Good News of peace to help you stand strong. And also use the shield of faith with which you can stop all the burning arrows of the Evil One. Accept God's salvation as your helmet, and take the sword of the Spirit, which is the word of God. Pray in the Spirit at all times with all kinds of prayers, asking for everything you need. To do this you must always be ready and never give up. Always pray for all God's people.

1 Thessalonians 5:16-18 (ESV): Rejoice always, pray without ceasing, give thanks in all circumstances; for this is the will of God in Christ Jesus for you.

Hebrews 13:5 (NKJV): Let your conduct be without covetousness; be content with such things as you have. For He Himself has said, "I will never leave you nor forsake you."

James 4:5-6 (TLB): Or what do you think the Scripture means when it says that the Holy Spirit, whom God has placed within us, watches over us with tender jealousy? But he gives us more and more strength to stand against all such evil longings. As the Scripture says, God gives strength to the humble but sets himself against the proud and haughty.

James 4:7 (NCV): So give yourselves completely to God. Stand against the devil, and the devil will run from you.

UNDERSTANDING

Psalm 32:8 (NIV): I will instruct you and teach you in the way you should go; I will counsel you with my loving eye on you.

Psalm 119:129-130 (MSG): Every word you give me is a miracle word—how could I help but obey? Break open your words, let the light shine out, let ordinary people see the meaning.

Proverbs 14:29 (NLT): People with understanding control their anger; a hot temper shows great foolishness.

Proverbs 19:21 (NLT): You can make many plans, but the LORD's purpose will prevail.

Isaiah 11:2 (ESV): And the Spirit of the Lord shall rest upon him, the Spirit of wisdom and understanding, the Spirit of counsel and might, the Spirit of knowledge and the fear of the Lord.

Jeremiah 33:3 (MSG): This is God's Message, the God who made earth, made it livable and lasting, known everywhere as God: "Call to me and I will answer you. I'll tell you marvelous and wondrous things that you could never figure out on your own."

1 Corinthians 13:12 (NIV): For now we see only a reflection as in a mirror; then we shall see face to face. Now I know in part; then I shall know fully, even as I am fully known.

Ephesians 1:17 (NCV): asking the God of our Lord Jesus Christ, the glorious Father, to give you a spirit of wisdom and revelation so that you will know him better.

WORSHIP AND PRAISE

Exodus 15:2 (NCV): The Lord gives me strength and makes me sing; he has saved me. He is my God, and I will praise him. He is the God of my ancestors, and I will honor him.

Exodus 23:25 (NKJV): So you shall serve the Lord your God, and He will bless your bread and your water. And I will take sickness away from the midst of you.

Deuteronomy 10: 12-15, 20-21 (TLB): And now, Israel, what does the Lord your God require of you except to listen carefully to all he says to you, and to obey for your own good the commandments I am giving you today, and to love him, and to worship him with all your hearts and souls? Earth and highest heaven belong to the Lord your God. And yet he rejoiced in your fathers and loved them so much that he chose you, their children, to be above every other nation, as is evident today ... You must fear the Lord your God and worship him and cling to him, and take oaths by his name alone. He is your praise and he is your God, the one who has done mighty miracles you yourselves have seen.

2 Samuel 6:5 (NCV): David and all the Israelites were celebrating in the presence of the Lord. They were playing wooden instruments: lyres, harps, tambourines, rattles, and cymbals.

2 Samuel 6:14-15 (NCV): Then David danced with all his might before the Lord. He had on a holy linen vest. David and all the Israelites shouted with joy and blew the trumpets as they brought the Ark of the Lord to the city.

Judges 5:3 (KJV): Hear, O ye kings; give ear, O ye princes; I, even I, will sing unto the LORD; I will sing praise to the LORD God of Israel.

2 Samuel 22:50 (NIV): Therefore I will praise you, Lord, among the nations; I will sing the praises of your name.

Psalm 68:4-5 (TLB): Sing praises to the Lord! Raise your voice in song to him who rides upon the clouds! Jehovah is his name—oh, rejoice in his presence. He is a father to the fatherless; he gives justice to the widows, for he is holy.

Psalm 103:1 (KJV): Bless the Lord, O my soul: and all that is within me, bless his holy name.

Psalm 138:1-3 (MSG): Thank you! Everything in me says "Thank you!" Angels listen as I sing my thanks. I kneel in worship facing your holy temple and say it again: "Thank you! Thank you for your love, thank you for your faithfulness; Most holy is your name, most holy is your Word. The moment I called out, you stepped in; you made my life large with strength."

Psalm 150:6 (NIV): Let everything that has breath praise the Lord. Praise the Lord.

Isaiah 25:1 (NIV): Lord, you are my God; I will exalt you and praise your name, for in perfect faithfulness you have done wonderful things, things planned long ago.

John 4:24 (NCV): God is spirit, and those who worship him must worship in spirit and truth.

Acts 16:25-26 (TLB): Around midnight, as Paul and Silas were praying and singing hymns to the Lord—and the other prisoners were listening— suddenly there was a great earthquake; the prison was shaken to its foundations, all the doors flew open—and the chains of every prisoner fell off!

A Letter from Jamey Santo

Dear Readers,

Thank you for coming on this journey of faith with me. Thank you for standing still in the storm that surrounds your life, and building your faith as you applied the principles and practical applications in these pages. I can tell you that the book you hold in your hands right now is a true labor of love. My deepest desire for you is that you discovered so many biblical truths you can use every day that you will see spiritual growth like you never have before! Whether you're on the mountaintop or in the lowest valley, you can experience peace and rest in the arms of Jesus with faith as your foundation, freedom and lifestyle. My personal hope is that this book will not be a one-time read for you, but will be a valuable tool you can use and reuse as you live out your faith daily. Turn to Chapter Ten whenever you need a booster shot of encouraging Scriptures to strengthen you. I know I will too!

Today, my family is still leaning on our faith in Jesus every day. Our older son, Preston is now eleven years old, and his love for Jesus (and his newly acquired sport, golf) shines through. Our sweet girl, Macey is four and brings us joy every day. Jeannie, the kids, and I still love playing and watching a good game of hoops. We look forward to getaways as a family, and opportunities to serve others everywhere we go.

As the ministry of Faith Builders Intl grows, we plan to help bring awareness and raise funds for pediatric brain tumor research, and bring the hope of Christ to families dealing with this horrendous disease.

You can help us by telling your family and friends about this book, giving copies as gifts, or spreading the word about Faith Builders Intl on your social media pages. If your church or ministry desires a special guest or conference speaker, reach out and I'd love to come and share more of our story and message in person. You can find me on Twitter, Instagram and Periscope at @jameysanto. Subscribe to our Faith Builders Youtube channel, or visit us on the web at www.faithbuildersintl.com. Check in often and see what's next on our journey, and please share yours with us. We'd love to hear from you.

Still in the Storm,
Jamey Santo

About Faith Builders International

Faith Builders International exists to serve churches, individuals, entrepreneurs, and families around the world, awakening them to the power of God's presence, purpose and plan. Through building faith, hope is restored, and love is extended. Our desire is to help build your faith to secure a stronger foundation for every season of your life. From tragedy to triumph, we are all called into a purpose, and hope is the pathway to that purpose. We extend love to our community and the world by partnering with missions and charitable organizations. You can find us online at www.faithbuildersintl.com. Sign up for our ministry updates as well as encouraging messages to help you keep faith as your foundation, your freedom, and your lifestyle. You can also find Jamey Santo's speaking schedule, discover new videos and blog posts, and interact with us. We want to connect with you!